THE POETRY OF ROBERT FROST

The Poetry of
ROBERT FROST

Edited by Edward Connery Lathem

I

IMPRINT SOCIETY

BARRE, MASSACHUSETTS, 1971

Copyright © 1969 by HOLT, RINEHART AND WINSTON, INC.
Copyright 1916, 1923, 1928, 1930, 1934, 1939, 1943,
1945, 1947, 1949, © 1967 by HOLT, RINEHART AND WINSTON, INC.
Copyright 1936, 1942, 1944, 1945, 1947, 1948, 1950,
1951, 1952, 1953, 1954, © 1955, 1956, 1958, 1959,
1960, 1961, 1962 by ROBERT FROST
Copyright © 1964, 1967, 1970 by LESLEY FROST BALLANTINE
Copyright © 1971 by THE IMPRINT SOCIETY, INC.

This printing of *The Poetry of Robert Frost* is published by special
arrangement with Holt, Rinehart and Winston, Inc. All rights
reserved, including the right to reproduce this book or portions
thereof in any form.

Library of Congress Catalog Card Number 70–142577
Standard Book Number 87636–013–4
PRINTED IN THE UNITED STATES OF AMERICA

Introduction

"My BEGINNINGS are lost in antiquity," Robert Frost told a gathering convened in his honor toward the close of his long life. "I began writing before anyone was aware of it₍. . .₎ in the high school, in the second year. And the first thing I wrote got published."[1] He was fond of reminiscing about that earliest literary impulse and about the circumstances associated with it, memories reaching back to Lawrence, Massachusetts, and a time early in 1890: "I was fifteen years old₍. . .₎. It was a dusty March day. I was coming home from high school, swinging my books in a strap. The thing kept going through my head."[2] "I recall how there was a wind and darkness. I had never written a poem before, and as I walked, it appeared like a revelation, and I became so taken by it that I was late to my grandmother's. The next day I took it to the editor of our school paper, and it was published."[3] This, his first poem, "La Noche Triste," appeared in the April 1890 issue of the *High School Bulletin*. Another of Robert Frost's memories of beginnings "lost in antiquity" was of his brief period as a Dartmouth College freshman and an occasion during the autumn of 1892 when, in the college library, he happened upon a copy of a magazine called *The Independent*: "₍. . .₎a magazine that I had never heard of, but it had a whole front page of poetry ₍. . .₎. And then over on the next page some, I think. And then I leafed over, and there was an editorial on the poem. That made a big impression on me. I didn't think that minute that I'll send something there, but that was where it grew on me

I'd send a poem there sometime. I don't know whether it came until I'd written the poem. Really, I can't remember that, but when I had the poem that I thought was a poem, I sent it there."[4] Thus it was that "My Butterfly," his first poem to appear in a publication of national circulation, came to be included in *The Independent* for November 8, 1894. "I just had it coming on me," he declared nearly sixty-five years later, speaking of that period when his career as a poet was getting underway. "I can't tell how it came, this wish to have something: write things and get them printed."[5] And he had recollections, too, of his decision to issue privately a little volume of his own verse, *Twilight*—consisting of five poems, including the one he had recently sold to *The Independent*: "I had two copies of Twilight printed and bound by a job printer in Lawrence Mass in 1894 probably out of pride in what Bliss Carmen and Maurice Thompson had said about the poem in it called My Butterfly. One copy I kept for myself and afterward destroyed. The other I gave away to a girl in St Lawrence University to show to her friends. It had no success and deserved none. But it unaccountably survived. . . . A few scattered lines in it are as much mine as any I was ever to write."[6]

The progress of Robert Frost's career, when fairly launched, was not to be swift. During a period of nearly two decades immediately following *The Independent's* acceptance of "My Butterfly" he averaged publication of barely one poem a year. It was not until 1913, while he and his family were temporarily living abroad, that his first regularly published book of verse, *A Boy's Will*, appeared in London, issued by David Nutt and Company, shortly after his thirty-ninth birthday. Less than a year later came *North of Boston* (London, 1914). Then, by the early months of 1915 both volumes were republished in America by Holt, and at last his reputation as a poet was established, a reputation that steadily grew throughout the next half-century. At his death in January 1963 Frost was without question his country's most-read, most-celebrated, most-beloved poet, and his poetry now constitutes a literary legacy, both to the present and to generations of readers yet to come.

*   *   *

In addition to his pre-eminence as a man of letters, Robert Frost was surely also among the best-printed of poets. He secured, as an observer well qualified to proffer such testimony once asserted, "to a degree unattained by any other ranking modern American author the devoted interest of his printers and publishers in making books worthy of what they have inside them."[7] And he himself had, always, a very special concern for and appreciation of design and production features of the many and various printings of his works over the years.

The first editions of *A Boy's Will* and *North of Boston*, each with its several binding variants, and the next-succeeding book, *Mountain Interval* (New York, 1916), were all volumes of relatively plain but decidedly pleasing and presentable character, both outside and in. (The fact is perhaps little known, in connection with the second book of this trio, that Frost's London publisher allowed for the presence of margins adequately wide and so proportioned that had sales been, as was hoped, substantial enough to render it feasible, decorative borders could have been added to the pages in subsequent printings of *North of Boston*.[8])

With *New Hampshire* (1923) and *West-Running Brook* (1928) the poet was personally responsible for bringing into his books the wood-engravings of J. J. Lankes—not intending them as illustrations of the poems, but rather as works of art that would stand on their own merit, ornamenting the volumes. After having discovered Lankes[9] and urged Henry Holt and Company to arrange for him to do at least three blocks for the then in preparation *New Hampshire*,[10] Frost— declaring, "Woodcuts are a form of art I'm the absolute victim of, and yours are such beautiful examples of it."—wrote graciously to the artist: "Just as most friendship is feigning, so is most liking a mere tacit understanding between A and B that A shall like B's work as much and as long as B likes A's. In our case I see good circumstantial evidence that there was no such sordid bargain. I liked your work before I knew you liked mine; you apparently liked mine somewhat before you knew I liked yours. Such a coincidence of taste can never be forgotten. It ought to settle it between us."[11] After *New Hampshire* had been published, and with friendship between the two men now rapidly developing, Frost wrote Lankes: "I'm proud of having thought of you for the book. People have all spoken of your part in it. We wont attempt to divide the honors, however, separating yours from mine. We'll hold them in common like true communists of the Golden Age, who talked no economics neither any sociology."[12] And five years later, of Lankes' accomplishment in *West-Running Brook,* he warmly commented: "Those are four beautiful pictures you did for the book—the one of the dead-alive tree especially—and they attach me to you, and make me wish for your society."[13]

Robert Frost's sixth book of new poetry, *A Further Range,* was issued in 1936. Typographically it was the creation of Joseph Blumenthal, the proprietor of The Spiral Press, who had half a dozen years earlier prepared Frost's first *Collected Poems* (1930). Early in 1930, as Frost and Blumenthal were just becoming acquainted through correspondence, and were discussing arrangements for going ahead with this initial collected edition, the poet confided engagingly: "You may not know it, but my sympathies have long been enlisted on the side of small presses and hand setting. My heart will be with you in your work."[14] Two weeks later, commenting on the foundry type (Lutetia) the printer had chosen for use in the book, he declared, "[. . .]I like this type so well and also the idea of the hand-setting so well that it would go against the latent craftsman in me to give them up."[15]

In six months' time *Collected Poems* was nearing completion, and an interesting sidelight is provided in further letters from the poet to Blumenthal at this period, the first written when plans were being made for including Frost's signature in the limited-edition copies: "I am limbering up my arm for all that autography. You agree with me that is the hardest job any of us have to do on the book, writing printing or publishing it."[16] And then, a few days thereafter he protested, with reference to the ordeal he had just undergone, and alluding to the royalty income he would receive per copy sold: "I'll never write autographs again for a dollar and a half apiece. It is too ignominious degrading and debilitating. Honestly."[17] Indeed, the signing of his various limited editions and printings—in quantities totaling, sometimes, as many as fifteen hundred copies—was a chore Frost accepted as inevitable, but always rather dreaded. On another occasion he wrote plaintively to Blumenthal: "The sheets have just gone back to you[. . .] I became a stranger to myself with the repetition of my name and now feel like the president of a bank none too solvent. Never mind. I observe the customs of my country."[18]

The Frost-Blumenthal relationship was for over three decades, within a context of warm and abiding personal friendship, an especially productive one. In succeeding years Blumenthal was responsible for *A Witness Tree* (1942), *Steeple Bush* (1947), the limited editions of both *A Masque of Reason* (1945) and *A Masque of Mercy* (1947), and for

the poet's final book, *In the Clearing*, published in 1962—
all of them singularly handsome volumes[19]—as well as for
a variety of special undertakings, including a distinguished
series of Frost's annual Christmas-poem booklets.

So well-printed did Robert Frost become, at the hands of
Joseph Blumenthal and others, and over so long a span of
years, that a survey today of the books, pamphlets, broadsides,
and other forms in which his works have been presented or
issued, reveals specimens of the achievements of a galaxy of
this country's leading graphic artists, designers, and printers
—numerous and impressive examples of distinguished book-
making and fine printing, representing such individuals, be-
sides Blumenthal and Lankes, as Daniel Berkeley Updike,
Bruce Rogers, James Chapin, W. A. Dwiggins, John O'Hara
Cosgrave II, Dard Hunter, Ray Nash, Thomas W. Nason,
Roderick D. Stinehour, Leonard Baskin, Peter Beilenson,
Fritz Eichenberg, P. J. Conkwright, and Joseph Low, to name
but a few.

* * *

The present edition of Robert Frost's poetry projects, in its
coverage, the poet's own intentions for the preparation of a
new major collection of his verse. Following the appearance
of *In the Clearing* in 1962, Mr. Frost spoke with the current
editor about such an undertaking and requested his assistance
with parts of the overall task. It was clear to the poet that the
volume would be constituted by adding the contents of *In the
Clearing* to that of *Complete Poems*, published in 1949. He
himself resolved, too, the matter of the title to be used. (He
had never, he indicated, really been happy with the designa-
tion of the 1949 book, which was by no means a complete
gathering even at the time of its issuance, and it had, of course,
inevitably become less complete with each new poem he

wrote.) Would not, he asked, with evident conviction as to its appropriateness, just *The Poetry of Robert Frost* be best?

When Mr. Frost's death in January of 1963 prevented his personally bringing the intended new collection into being, the responsibility for doing so devolved upon his publishers and estate (the two being effectively joined under the poet's will, wherein he had named his friend who headed the firm of Holt, Rinehart and Winston to be his estate's sole executor and trustee). From the outset several basic requirements for the book were obvious to those concerned with its planning. First, it must maintain the tradition of typographic excellence so long associated with Frost volumes. Happily, the accomplishment of this was fully assured by the agreement of Rudolph Ruzicka, internationally celebrated typographer and dean of America's graphic artists, to serve as designer—and, not incidentally, by the selection of Mr. Ruzicka's types Fairfield and Fairfield Medium to be used for setting the text.

Secondly, although in all of Holt's previous comprehensive editions of Robert Frost's poetry the scheme followed had been to accord a new page for the opening of each poem, this would now manifestly be unfeasible, for to have followed the *Complete Poems* format and simply to have added the pages necessary to accommodate the poems of *In the Clearing,* plus an index and slightly enlarged front matter, would have meant producing a book of well over seven hundred and fifty pages —undesirable in terms of both bulk and cost. Actually, ample precedent existed, if precedent were required, of the author's having himself sanctioned his poems' being "run-on" in their publication. Several editions during his lifetime had embodied that feature, beginning with the earliest volume of his *Selected Poems* (1923) and including the English *Complete Poems* in 1951. An attempted assessment, moreover, of the reaction of readers seemed to suggest that those who might feel

xiii

that a two-line poem, for instance, on an otherwise blank page could have positive aesthetic force and significance were counterbalanced by other persons who firmly held that such was an awkward, wasteful, even ridiculous arrangement.

A third fundamental conclusion was that there would be no critical introduction in the volume, nor would Mr. Frost's essay "The Figure a Poem Makes" (which had been used as a preface in several editions, from the time of Holt's 1939 *Collected Poems* onward) be included.[20] Similarly, interpretive notes were to be avoided.[21] But it was felt that scholars, particularly, might value the availability of certain bibliographical information[22] and data on textual variations among the principal printed versions of the poetry.

The editor's assignment from the Frost Estate was to prepare an edition that would serve both general readers and scholarly users. Although upon but casual consideration it might not seem that the needs of the two groups should be markedly dissimilar, it was in fact found that circumstances of past publication and Frost's attitude toward his text were such that at least the general reader would oftentimes be helpfully served by some degree of editorial attention to the poems. The decision was made, therefore, that this new collection, planned for publication in 1969, would be an edited one. It would, however, include within its notes section precise indication of all textual emendations by the editor. Thus, the desired objective could be attained of editorially enhancing textual clarity, while at the same time flagging every such change (dealing mostly with punctuation, and including some reversions to earlier, correct forms of what were in effect corruptions within the two basic copy-texts), so that scholars and others could readily know just which readings reflected editor's alterations.

Mr. Frost was, in many ways, a very inconsistent person—

as Emerson proclaims great souls are wont to be.[23] (It was, withal, one of the myriad fascinating aspects of his personality.) In some respects he cared a great deal about fine points of textual detail; in others, he was indifferent, if not actually perverse or cavalier, regarding them. His letters to his publishers and printers echo over and again the hope that his text would emerge, in book after book, as correct as possible. Yet he felt uneasy about, and shrank from, the responsibility of accomplishing that end himself. "I like an exact text as much as anybody," he wrote in 1930, while preparing his *Collected Poems* for the press, "but I should hate to have it left too much to me to achieve one. I reread my own poems, when I have to, with a kind of shrinking eye that doesnt see very well. I doubt if it's inattention I suffer from. It may be love-blindness."[24] And to another correspondent, who queried him, after the 1930 edition had appeared, about evident deficiencies of punctuation therein, he replied disarmingly: "[. . .]I indulge a sort of indifference to punctuation. I dont mean I despise it. I value it. But I seem rather willing to let other people look after it for me."[25]

Although, by and large, Frost did not actually relish having individuals challenge him regarding the punctuation of his verse, any more than he appreciated being questioned about substantive elements of the poems, he sometimes did respond positively and appreciatively to corrective inquiry. Prof. George F. Whicher of Amherst College entertainingly told, many years ago, of such an instance: "When 'The White-tailed Hornet' appeared in the *Yale Review,* my wife and I were absurdly perplexed by a line which then read:

> To err is human, not to animal.

Was *to* a misprint for *too*? Had an essential word been omitted? Could *to animal* conceivably be taken as an infinitive?

The simple explanation eluded us as the obvious sometimes will, but that night my wife woke up from a sound sleep repeating the line with an intonation that cleared up the difficulty. We laughed with Frost over how we had been stumped, and for the sake of other dunderheads he printed the line in *A Further Range*:

> To err is human, not to, animal.

If there can be," the professor concluded his anecdote, "Halley's comet, why not Whicher's comma—or in this case, Mrs. Whicher's, since she suggested it? All book-gazers are hereby notified."[26]

In somewhat like manner, the present editor a decade and a half ago, in doing a special separate edition of the poem "New Hampshire,"[27] had occasion to make a number of textual queries of Mr. Frost, including one in a passage which within the copy-text (*Complete Poems*) read:

> 'You hear those hound-dogs sing on Moosilauke?
> Well they remind me of the hue and cry
> We've heard against the Mid-Victorians

In the second line as given, "Well" is apparently an adverb, descriptive of the manner in which or the degree to which the dogs remind the speaker of the hue and cry that has been raised—a grammatical construction equivalent to the second line of "The Vantage Point":

> Well I know where to hie me—in the dawn,

or the twelfth line of "The Demiurge's Laugh":

> And well I knew what the Demon meant.

In fact, this was not the poet's intended sense at all, as might possibly be guessed through assessing the tone of the dialogue itself, but as could definitely be known by hearing Mr. Frost read the line. "Well" is in reality an interjection, and it decidedly requires a comma to make plain that it is to be read as such. The author, on having his attention called to the matter, after more than thirty years of its standing otherwise in book upon book, promptly indicated that the change should be made:

> Well, they remind me of the hue and cry
> We've heard against the Mid-Victorians

Another of the alterations authorized at this same time, to record but one more, was the simple insertion of a comma at the end of the second of the following three lines of "New Hampshire":

> Just specimens is all New Hampshire has,
> One each of everything as in a showcase,
> Which naturally she doesn't care to sell.

In its version as emended by the poet, the passage is, of course, made unequivocally to convey the sense that it is its specimens, not the showcase, which the state does not choose to sell.

When Mr. Frost talked about preparing the volume that was to be *The Poetry of Robert Frost*, one of the things foremost in his mind was a desire to comb out any British spellings which might still exist within the text of his first two books and which ought to be replaced with American forms. In the event, this proved to be an area of no problem at all, and corrections in orthography were associated more with other things. Proper names had been a minor bogey in the past. (Vilhjalmur Stefansson was for years, prior to ultimate correction, cited as "Steffanson," and Eugene O'Neill became

"O'Neil" in the early printings of *Complete Poems*.) For the new book, "Hackluyt" was corrected to "Hakluyt" in the subtitle of "The Discovery of the Madeiras," and the reading "Georges Bank" (an area of ocean shelf providing excellent fishing grounds off the New England coast) was restored to the poem entitled "The Flower Boat," in place of the corruption "George's bank" which had badly obscured the reference. Also, the spelling of the orchid genus *"Cypripedium"* was changed from *"Cyprepedium,"* even though the incorrect spelling was present in dialogue, on the grounds that there could be no difference in the word's pronunciation ("Langshang" on the other hand, although wrong, was not altered within its context of dialogue to "Langshan" since the two word-endings are quite differently said). Another phase of editorial attention to spellings involved normalizing such variants as "dye stuff" of *A Further Range* and "dyestuff" of *In the Clearing*, "meter" and "metre," "offense" and "offence," "ax" and "axe," "shan't" and "sha'n't."

Diverse spellings and irregularity of practice in punctuation are not, of course, apt to render text unintelligible, but they can distract, puzzle, and indeed annoy readers, undesirably intruding upon an assimilation of what the author has wished to communicate. A reader will most readily grasp the meaning of text in which spelling and punctuation are consistently styled. Since Robert Frost's first and last books were published nearly half a century apart, it seemed desirable to have as one of the objectives of the projected 1969 edition the attainment of a reasonable consistency in the styling of both spelling and punctuation—to have this styling represent usage at the close of Mr. Frost's career. This involved eliminating, for example, the heavy employment of hyphens to form words that in current usage would normally appear as either single or separate words. Although, obviously, there was need to exercise care

to avoid altering hyphenization where it was really signifi-
cant from the standpoint of sense or some feature of the poet's
deliberate artistic intent, it would be hard to defend, on either
practical or aesthetic grounds, that whereas "childlike" was
satisfactory as employed in the copy-text, there was reason to
retain hyphens in such words as "star-like" or "business-like"
or the rather absurd "unship-like." And it is questionable also,
to cite one further example, that it is helpful to readers to
perpetuate the hyphenated form in the following passage from
"Birches":

> [· · ·]when Truth broke in
> With all her matter-of-fact[. . .]

Here the term hyphenated is surely akin to that which appears
in a line from "On the Heart's Beginning to Cloud the Mind"
which in the copy-text reads:

> Matter of fact has made them brave.

and not to that of the term as adverbially used in this passage
in the copy-text's version of "One More Brevity":

> In spite of the way his tail had smacked
> My floor so hard and matter-of-fact.

Similarly, with respect to commas, the line from "Stopping
by Woods on a Snowy Evening" which the copy-text carries as:

> His house is in the village though;

is perfectly intelligible as it stands, and it could be passed over
just as it is, without the editorial insertion of a comma before
"though" in this adverbial element. Yet to emend the line to:

> His house is in the village, though;

does seem in order, not out of deference to any rules, but
because the comma's absence is divergent from a style pattern

the reader has elsewhere encountered within the copy-text volume, in lines of similar construction such as these:

It's seldom I get down except for meals, though.

That's always the way with the blueberries, though:

You can see what is troubling Granny, though.

I tell them they can't get me through the door, though:

This is not sorrow, though;[. . .]

Unfortunately all of one kind, though.

Therefore, the absence of a comma before "though" in the "Stopping by Woods . . ." line would be a difference which might claim the reader's consciousness, if only vaguely or momentarily so, distracting him from the text.

In this same poem another editorial consideration presents itself in a line which in the copy-text reads:

The woods are lovely, dark and deep[. . .]

As punctuated, "dark and deep" may be taken as in apposition to "lovely," defining the quality or character of the woods' loveliness. Or, alternatively, it is at least suggested that a pause in reading is intended after "lovely"—and that these are not simply adjectives given in series, which could be punctuated "lovely, dark, and deep." However, investigation reveals that in what appears to be the first-draft manuscript of the poem, Mr. Frost wrote the line:[28]

The woods are lovely dark and deep

and such utter lack of punctuation would seem to suggest he intended all three adjectives to have equal weight or stress. This supposition is further supported by evidence of the first appearance of the poem in a magazine, prior to book publication. There the phrase is exactly as it is in the apparent first draft, with no commas at all: "lovely dark and deep."[29] (This unorthodox practice of wholly omitting punctuation for co-ordinate words in series is something the poet indulged in in his letters, and occasionally even in his books.[30]) But conclusive evidence regarding the manner in which the line should be read (and, accordingly, how it should be punctuated) is provided by the manner in which the poet himself, in fact, said the line. Fortunately, there is in this respect no need to rely on memory, for literally scores of voice recordings exist of Frost saying his poems.[31] Over and over again he is heard to give the three adjectives approximately equal stress, with no vocal suggestion that punctuation other than:

> The woods are lovely, dark, and deep[. . .]

would be appropriate.

It is highly significant that with Robert Frost an editor undertaking textual criticism has, in a fashion and to a degree that has doubtless never before obtained with regard to one of our major poets, an opportunity to draw not just upon manuscript and printed sources, but also upon a vast body of oral evidence as well. In the poem "The Death of the Hired Man," to provide another example, simple in character, the opening has in all of Mr. Frost's books heretofore appeared:

> Mary sat musing on the lamp-flame at the table
> Waiting for Warren.[. . .]

which a reader might well take as indicating that the table, set for a meal about to be partaken of, was awaiting Warren's coming, rather than that it was Mary who was waiting. Such a reading makes sense and is an interpretation that could be adhered to, but the oral evidence provided by Mr. Frost himself makes it unmistakably plain that a comma is really appropriate after "table":

> Mary sat musing on the lamp-flame at the table,
> Waiting for Warren. [. . .]

Recordings that preserve Frost's own manner of saying his poems can frequently be used to remove ambiguity or bafflement arising from the poet's indifference to punctuation. Often, as has been suggested, absence or irregularity of punctuation is not so much an absolute difficulty as it is merely a deterrent to immediate comprehension. The following are a few examples of lines in which the commas have been supplied by the present editor, but which unpunctuated would be potentially troublesome:

> A bead of silver water more or less,
> Strung on your hair, won't hurt your summer looks.

> Though as for that, the passing there
> Had worn them really about the same[. . .]

> "But why, when no one wants you to, go on?

> As far as I can see, this autumn haze

Certain areas of editorial concern in preparing *The Poetry of Robert Frost* have related to problems arising more from prior typographical, than literary, styling—or the absence thereof. In the matter of quote marks, for example, *Complete Poems,* one of the two copy-texts for this edition, uses single quotes for the opening of quotations and double quotes for quotations within quotations. Some readers in observing this have assumed it to be an extension of British practice imposed upon Mr. Frost's first two books when initially published in London in 1913 and 1914. Actually, although *A Boy's Will*

THE BEAR

The bear puts both arms around the tree above her
And draws it down as if it were a lover
And its choke cherries lips to kiss good-by,
Then lets it snap back upright in the sky.
Her next step rocks a boulder on the wall.————————5
(She's making her cross-country in the fall).
Her great weight creaks the barbed wire in its staples
As she flings over and off down through the maples,
Leaving on one wire tooth a lock of hair.
Such is the uncaged progress of the bear.————————10
The world has room to make a bear feel free;
The universe seems cramped to you and me.
Man acts more like the poor bear in a cage
That all day fights a nervous inward rage,
His mood rejecting all his mind suggests.————————15
He paces back and forth and never rests
The toe-nail click and shuffle of his feet,
The telescope at one end of his beat,
And at the other end the microscope,
Two instruments of nearly equal hope,————————20
And in conjunction giving quite a spread.
Or if he rests from scientific tread,
'Tis only to sit back and sway his head
Through ninety odd degrees of arc, it seems,
Between two metaphysical extremes.————————25
He sits back on his fundamental butt
With lifted snout and eyes (if any) shut,
(He almost looks religious but he's not),
And back and forth he sways from cheek to cheek,
At one extreme agreeing with one Greek,————————30
At the other agreeing with another Greek

[347]

Copy-text page (from *Complete Poems 1949*) showing
emendations and other markings by the Editor, as made
in preparing *The Poetry of Robert Frost* for publication.

did follow such form, *North of Boston* from the beginning used double quotes to begin quotations and single quotes for internal ones, and the advent of what has been, thus, mistakenly regarded as merely a continuation of English usage in quotation did not come into Frost's books on a comprehensive basis until the 1930 edition of *Collected Poems*. It was therein a typographical refinement preferred by the book's designer,[32] and it has since been followed in all collected editions until the present volume.[33]

A further practice traceable to 1930's *Collected Poems* is the using of a short dash (–), rather than a full one-em dash (—), a typographical feature quite satisfactory in both the 1930 and 1939 collected editions,[34] where the dash employed was heavy in appearance and evidently was given a slight amount of spacing on either side. But in later books, where the short or three-quarter-em dash used does not have these characteristics, it is far less effective for places in which a dash is intended to represent abrupt changes of thought or other breaks of continuity in sentence structure. A rather objectionable innovation of the 1930 edition, which has also long been perpetuated, is the elimination of the double or two-em dash (——) and the substitution for it of the short dash. In the present edition the more acceptable pre-1930 usage has been reverted to, since the double dash is a recognized standard means of indicating interruption in dialogue.

Other errors that have sometimes in the past crept into the selected and collected editions have resulted from a failure by proofreaders, including the poet himself, to realize that provision of interlinear space (for various purposes of separation) had been omitted in the re-setting of poems. These mistakes often came about because in the printed versions used as copy-texts a line preceding the point at which extra interlinear space would normally have been desired had, as it happened, come at the bottom of a page. Thus, the printer, given no special instructions that additional line-spacing was required there, provided none, and if after the new setting of the poem the line in question did not again fall at the end of a page, the needed interlinear space was quite apt to be wanting. This result could be particularly damaging to dialogue. For instance, in the following passage early in the poem "Build Soil" the absence of spacing after the first line, which in the poem's original appearance in *A Further Range* was at the bottom of page eighty-six, makes it seem, as printed in collected and selected editions in 1939, 1946, 1949, 1955, and 1963, that all this text is uttered by one speaker, Tityrus:

> I doubt if you're convinced the times are bad.
> I keep my eye on Congress, Meliboeus.
> They're in the best position of us all
> To know if anything is very wrong.
> I mean they could be trusted to give the alarm[. . .]

However, careful (and, of course, disconcerting to a reader) analysis of the dialogue which immediately precedes this will reveal—as manuscript evidence sustains[35]—the first line is not Tityrus's at all, but is spoken by the other character in the poem, Meliboeus.

An organizational inconsistency of the *Complete Poems* copy-text, corrected in the 1969 edition, is the inclusion of part-titles and other indications of the units into which the later, but not the earlier, of Mr. Frost's individual books were divided. *Collected Poems* of 1930 was so planned that the original sectional arrangements of the five books it brought together (*A Boy's Will* through *West-Running Brook*) were not identified at all. However, the 1939 collected edition, in adding the *A Further Range* poems, reproduced the part-titles and the breakdown of the table of contents of *A Further*

Range, exactly as they had appeared in that book—a practice continued, with respect to subsequent books, in the succeeding comprehensive editions. Such features are not represented in the main body of *The Poetry of Robert Frost* (in reversion to the 1930 scheme), but are, rather, described in detail within notes devoted to the separate books of the total collection.

The foregoing is suggestive of some of the considerations which confronted the editor in his preparation of this 1969 edition, *The Poetry of Robert Frost,* now handsomely issued anew by The Imprint Society. Working under the authority of those responsible for administering Mr. Frost's literary interests, he attempted to accomplish their established goal of bringing forth a volume having as great a degree of accuracy and clarity of text as possible—a purpose based on a recognition of the substantial lack of careful textual scrutiny which had characterized Frost editions in the past[36] and, also, on the poet's known desire to have any new collection at this juncture subjected to a thorough review of its text. The editor's assigned task was *to edit:* to proceed with care, restraint, and conviction—operating within a scope of limited range, using restricted means, being neither inflexible nor yet erratic or casual in the exercise of critical attention and editorial treatment—and acting on the basis of having gathered from manuscript, printed, and oral sources as much textual evidence as possible (but very little of which, because of space limitations, could be reflected in the book's notes). Such was the aim and effort.

Had Mr. Frost lived to preside over the creation of this comprehensive volume, it would undoubtedly have had differences from the present book. It might have included a few new poems (as *Complete Poems* had done back in 1949). It possibly would have carried, too, an introductory essay by the poet. It almost surely would not have featured bibliographical notes or indications of variant readings. And clearly there would have been no need for the citing of emendations within it, since these would have been changes, whether verbal or punctuational, which the author could freely have made (as indeed he had in earlier editions)[37] without any declaration whatsoever, while it has of course been proper for the editor to record minutely herein each and all of his alterations of any kind. It is hoped, however, that *The Poetry of Robert Frost,* conservatively edited as a book for both the general reader and the scholar, and as an interim provision against the time when a variorum or definitive edition is prepared, will prove to be both a useful and a convenient volume.

The editor has in his work had the advantage of, and is most grateful for, the full co-operation and counsel of the Robert Frost Estate, as well as the assistance of several individuals having special qualification to advise him on matters associated with the textual review of Mr. Frost's verse. For this he tenders his warmest thanks.

EDWARD CONNERY LATHEM

NOTES

1. RF speaking in New York City, January 16, 1958, at a dinner of the Poetry Society of America; tape recording, Amherst College Library.
2. RF quoted by Gardner Jackson in "I Will Teach Only When I Have Something to Tell," *The Boston Sunday Globe*, November 23, 1924, Editorial Section, p. 3.
3. RF quoted by John Sherrill in "A Strange Kind of Laziness," *Guideposts*, August 1955, p. 3.
4. RF quoted by Edward Connery Lathem in "Freshman Days . . .," *Dartmouth Alumni Magazine*, March 1959, p. 20.
5. *Ibid.*
6. RF in an inscription to Earle J. Bernheimer, dated February 1, 1940, in the sole extant copy of *Twilight*, now preserved within the collection formed by C. Waller Barrett at the University of Virginia Library.
7. Ray Nash in "Robert Frost and His Printers," *The Book Collector's Packet*, January 1946, p. 10.
8. RF himself occasionally alluded to this provision by Nutt, and Nash, *op. cit.*, mentions it (p. 11), but without specific reference to RF as his source of information.
9. Ray Nash in "Meeting of Mounted Men," *Print*, Spring 1942, pp. 63–[64], and Loring Holmes Dodd's *Celebrities at Our Hearthside* (Boston: Dresser, Chapman & Grimes, 1959), pp. 39–40, both treat of RF's "discovery" of Lankes' work.
10. RF to Lincoln MacVeagh, undated card, postmarked July 28, 1923; The Jones Library, Amherst, Massachusetts.
11. RF to J. J. Lankes, undated letter, postmarked August 20, [1923]; University of Texas Library.
12. RF to J. J. Lankes, letter dated December 31, 1923; University of Texas Library.

13. RF to J. J. Lankes, letter dated December 22, 1928; University of Texas Library.

   The *West-Running Brook* wood-engraving depicting "the dead-alive tree," to which RF here refers, was ever a particular favorite of his. The original block, given him by Lankes, was to the end of the poet's life a possession he cherished and accorded a place of honor on the fireplace mantle in his living room.

14. RF to Joseph Blumenthal, letter dated February 18, 1930; Amherst College Library.

15. RF to Joseph Blumenthal, letter dated March 4, 1930; Amherst College Library.

16. RF to Joseph Blumenthal, letter dated September 4, 1930; Amherst College Library.

17. RF to Joseph Blumenthal, letter dated September 9, 1930; Amherst College Library.

18. RF to Joseph Blumenthal, letter dated April 21, 1936, relating to the limited issuance of *A Further Range* (eight hundred and three copies); Amherst College Library.

19. In each of these cases, except the two *Masques,* the trade printings were done outside The Spiral Press, from plates of the pages supplied by Blumenthal. The trade editions of the *Masques* were from settings of type entirely distinct from the Blumenthal limited editions.

   Among RF's tributes to Blumenthal, reflecting the poet's great appreciation of the bookmaking achievements of his printer-friend, is this passage from a letter, dated April 28, 1942 (original preserved within the Dartmouth College Library), written just after the publication of *A Witness Tree:* "Again your art and my art go hand in hand to market without rivalry. We'll hope they'll say we're both better than ever.[. . .] I'd be inclined to doubt if any writer in our time has had such a string of beautiful books as you have made me. Your respect for my poetry has done a lot I am sure to win it the respect of other people."

20. "The Figure a Poem Makes" was included among other of RF's introductions and prose writings in the volume entitled *Selected Prose of Robert Frost,* edited by Hyde Cox and Ed-

ward Connery Lathem, published some three years after the poet's death (New York: Holt, Rinehart and Winston, 1966).

21. RF frequently professed an aversion to annotative interpretation of his poems (despite the fact that in his public readings he would himself often explicitly provide such annotation, orally). On one occasion (May 18, 1953) before a Dartmouth College audience he declared, referring to a term used in his poetry, "I'm afraid somebody'll have to write a footnote on that for me sometime, and I'll turn over in my grave if they do—I'll start revolving in my grave."

22. The still-standard bibliographical volume, compiled by W. B. Shubrick Clymer and Charles R. Green, entitled *Robert Frost: A Bibliography,* was at the time of the poet's death over a quarter of a century out of date, having been published at Amherst, Massachusetts, by The Jones Library in 1937.

23. Ralph Waldo Emerson in "Self-Reliance," *Essays,* First Series (Boston: James Munroe, 1841), p. 47: "With consistency a great soul has simply nothing to do."

    RF was, indeed, not merely inconsistent, he was in his nature self-contradictory. Theodore Morrison in the opening sentence of his article "The Agitated Heart" wrote, penetratively, of RF: "The only way to describe a man so complex as Robert Frost is to say that he was a bundle of paradoxes, that he was made up of pairs of opposites, both of which were true of him at the same time." (*The Atlantic Monthly,* July 1967, p. 72.)

24. RF to Joseph Blumenthal, undated letter; Amherst College Library.

    In periods of concern about textual details the poet evidently made a number of attempts to keep track of changes or corrections he desired to have introduced into new editions, by maintaining copies of his books into which were entered manuscript emendations. Although these volumes, through loss or otherwise, usually did not long survive as continuing records, the present editor had two of RF's annotated copies of the 1939 *Collected Poems* placed in his hands when he began the task of preparing *The Poetry of Robert Frost* for publication. They are now preserved in the Dartmouth College Library.

25. RF to Leonidas W. Payne Jr., undated letter; *Selected Letters of Robert Frost*, edited by Lawrance Thompson (New York: Holt, Rinehart and Winston, 1964), p. 370.

Another of RF's attitudes toward punctuation, at variance with the observation just quoted, is revealed by his remarks to an audience at Dartmouth College on May 8, 1951— remarks that prefaced a little anecdote about the importance of punctuation: "I hate to depend on punctuation at all. I hate to end with a word in one sentence that might well belong to the next sentence. I got that from writing telegrams. I hate to write the word 'stop' in a telegram. You want it to stop itself."

26. George F. Whicher in a letter published in "The Crow's Nest" column, *The Colophon*, New Series, Autumn 1937, p. 618.

27. *New Hampshire: A Poem by Robert Frost* (Hanover, New Hampshire: The New Dresden Press, 1955), "limited to 750 numbered copies signed by the author."

28. The last three stanzas of the apparent first-draft manuscript of "Stopping by Woods on a Snowy Evening" are reproduced in facsimile in *Preface to Poetry* by Charles W. Cooper and John Holmes (New York: Harcourt, Brace, 1946), p. [604].

29. This first appearance of the poem was in *The New Republic*, March 7, 1923, p. 47. Immediately thereafter "Stopping by Woods . . ." was published in England in the April 1923 number of *The Chapbook*, p. 3, where the phrase was also printed as "lovely dark and deep."

30. As examples of such omission by RF of commas in personal correspondence, see the quotations herein from his letters of September 4 and 9, 1930, to Joseph Blumenthal (Notes 16 and 17). Among a number of similar instances in his published poems may be cited, as included within *Complete Poems*, "I Will Sing You One-O" (lines 74 and 75), "The Egg and the Machine" (lines 13 and 14), or "Something for Hope" (line 6).

31. The largest collection of such recordings is maintained at the Amherst College Library. It was assembled there principally through the initiative and efforts of Dr. Jack W. C. Hagstrom.

32. Joseph Blumenthal in conversation with the present editor, November 15, 1970.

33. This practice was evidently experimental on Joseph Blumenthal's part, and it was not regarded by him as adequately satisfactory to be adopted as a standard. It did not become the house style of The Spiral Press, and it was never thereafter used by Blumenthal himself in any of his volumes of new poetry by RF. Ironically, all of Holt's subsequent collected and selected editions and the Modern Library edition of *Poems* in 1946 (none of which was designed by Blumenthal) were made to conform to the 1930 manner of setting off quotations.

34. Actually, the last book only (*A Further Range*) of the 1939 *Collected Poems* does use full one-em dashes. This divergence of typographical practice within the 1939 edition is explained by the fact that the rest of the volume was done from printing plates of the 1930 edition, whereas the final unit, incorporating the one book of new Frost poems to be published in the 1930–39 interval, was set (except for poem titles) in type different from that employed nine years before and had, also, other variant features of composition.

35. For example, a draft manuscript of "Build Soil" at The Jones Library substantiates RF's intention of a break at this point in the poem, signifying a shift of speakers in the dialogue.

36. Although RF confessed (Note 24) with respect to the checking over of his text, "I reread my own poems, when I have to, with a kind of shrinking eye," and despite the fact that he had in general little taste for proofreading or sustained efforts to attain either consistency or other features of textual reform for his poetry, neither did his publishers, apparently, regard themselves as empowered to initiate even minor textual alterations or feel disposed to urge such changes upon the poet. Evidence of this is provided by instances in which the absence of punctuation, originally eliminated through wear or breakage of type characters, has in succeeding editions been faithfully, if sometimes preposterously, maintained—perhaps in keeping with the dictum of Benbow, "Poets, however, are to spell, capitalize, and punctuate (or not) as fancy moves

them." (John Benbow, *Manuscript & Proof* (New York: Oxford University Press, 1937), p. 75.) Of the multiple cases that might be cited in which broken-away periods and commas, obviously required by the sense of the text, have gone uncorrected for many years, perhaps the most startling act of fidelity to a faulty copy-text occurs in the 1963 *Selected Poems*. Following 1949's *Complete Poems,* the 1963 edition (issued by RF's publishers shortly after his death) takes obvious pains to ensure that a comma does not appear after the second word in this phrase from line 157 of the poem "A Hundred Collars": "No, no no, thank you." What was not recognized, however, in thus carefully mirroring the 1949 punctuation is that in *Complete Poems* the missing comma (present in all previous editions) has manifestly been broken off, since a space actually exists for it where it should appear, this in addition to the presence there of normal word-spacing: "No, no no, thank you."

37. Notes in this edition, treating individual poems of the overall collection, give in their entries for VARIANTS evidence of certain of RF's verbal changes in his poems.

In this connection, the poet once commented to an individual closely concerned with his life and works: "I'm glad you think my changes are improvements. Of course I never held that nothing could be done about a poem once it was written. When I am coordinating well (in good form mentally and physically) I notice I falter in the verse very little and get in my best strokes as I go.ᵣ. . .ᵢ" (RF to Robert S. Newdick, letter dated June 10, 1935; Library of Congress.)

Contents

Contents

WEST-RUNNING BROOK

A FURTHER RANGE

xlvii

1

The Poetry of Robert Frost

THE PASTURE

I'm going out to clean the pasture spring;
I'll only stop to rake the leaves away
(And wait to watch the water clear, I may):
I shan't be gone long.—You come too.

I'm going out to fetch the little calf
That's standing by the mother. It's so young
It totters when she licks it with her tongue.
I shan't be gone long.—You come too.

1

A Boy's Will

: 1913 :

INTO MY OWN

One of my wishes is that those dark trees,
So old and firm they scarcely show the breeze,
Were not, as 'twere, the merest mask of gloom,
But stretched away unto the edge of doom.

I should not be withheld but that some day   5
Into their vastness I should steal away,
Fearless of ever finding open land,
Or highway where the slow wheel pours the sand.

I do not see why I should e'er turn back,
Or those should not set forth upon my track   10
To overtake me, who should miss me here
And long to know if still I held them dear.

They would not find me changed from him they knew—
Only more sure of all I thought was true.

GHOST HOUSE

I dwell in a lonely house I know
That vanished many a summer ago,
    And left no trace but the cellar walls,
    And a cellar in which the daylight falls
And the purple-stemmed wild raspberries grow.   5

O'er ruined fences the grapevines shield
The woods come back to the mowing field;
    The orchard tree has grown one copse

5

Of new wood and old where the woodpecker chops;
The footpath down to the well is healed.   10

I dwell with a strangely aching heart
In that vanished abode there far apart
   On that disused and forgotten road
   That has no dust-bath now for the toad.
Night comes; the black bats tumble and dart;   15

The whippoorwill is coming to shout
And hush and cluck and flutter about:
   I hear him begin far enough away
   Full many a time to say his say
Before he arrives to say it out.   20

It is under the small, dim, summer star.
I know not who these mute folk are
   Who share the unlit place with me—
   Those stones out under the low-limbed tree
Doubtless bear names that the mosses mar.   25

They are tireless folk, but slow and sad—
Though two, close-keeping, are lass and lad—
   With none among them that ever sings,
   And yet, in view of how many things,
As sweet companions as might be had.   30

MY NOVEMBER GUEST

My Sorrow, when she's here with me,
   Thinks these dark days of autumn rain
Are beautiful as days can be;
She loves the bare, the withered tree;
   She walks the sodden pasture lane.   5

6

Her pleasure will not let me stay.
  She talks and I am fain to list:
She's glad the birds are gone away,
She's glad her simple worsted gray
  Is silver now with clinging mist.   10

The desolate, deserted trees,
  The faded earth, the heavy sky,
The beauties she so truly sees,
She thinks I have no eye for these,
  And vexes me for reason why.   15

Not yesterday I learned to know
  The love of bare November days
Before the coming of the snow,
But it were vain to tell her so,
  And they are better for her praise.   20

LOVE AND A QUESTION

A Stranger came to the door at eve,
  And he spoke the bridegroom fair.
He bore a green-white stick in his hand,
  And, for all burden, care.
He asked with the eyes more than the lips   5
  For a shelter for the night,
And he turned and looked at the road afar
  Without a window light.

The bridegroom came forth into the porch
  With, "Let us look at the sky,   10
And question what of the night to be,
  Stranger, you and I."
The woodbine leaves littered the yard,

7

The woodbine berries were blue,
Autumn, yes, winter was in the wind;   15
  "Stranger, I wish I knew."

Within, the bride in the dusk alone
  Bent over the open fire,
Her face rose-red with the glowing coal
  And the thought of the heart's desire.   20
The bridegroom looked at the weary road,
  Yet saw but her within,
And wished her heart in a case of gold
  And pinned with a silver pin.

The bridegroom thought it little to give   25
  A dole of bread, a purse,
A heartfelt prayer for the poor of God,
  Or for the rich a curse;
But whether or not a man was asked
  To mar the love of two   30
By harboring woe in the bridal house,
  The bridegroom wished he knew.

A LATE WALK

When I go up through the mowing field,
  The headless aftermath,
Smooth-laid like thatch with the heavy dew,
  Half closes the garden path.

And when I come to the garden ground,   5
  The whir of sober birds
Up from the tangle of withered weeds
  Is sadder than any words.

A tree beside the wall stands bare,
  But a leaf that lingered brown,   10
Disturbed, I doubt not, by my thought,
  Comes softly rattling down.

I end not far from my going forth,
  By picking the faded blue
Of the last remaining aster flower   15
  To carry again to you.

STARS

How countlessly they congregate
  O'er our tumultuous snow,
Which flows in shapes as tall as trees
  When wintry winds do blow!—

As if with keenness for our fate,   5
  Our faltering few steps on
To white rest, and a place of rest
  Invisible at dawn—

And yet with neither love nor hate,
  Those stars like some snow-white   10
Minerva's snow-white marble eyes
  Without the gift of sight.

STORM FEAR

When the wind works against us in the dark,
And pelts with snow
The lower-chamber window on the east,
And whispers with a sort of stifled bark,
The beast,   5

9

"Come out! Come out!"—
It costs no inward struggle not to go,
Ah, no!
I count our strength,
Two and a child,   10
Those of us not asleep subdued to mark
How the cold creeps as the fire dies at length—
How drifts are piled,
Dooryard and road ungraded,
Till even the comforting barn grows far away,   15
And my heart owns a doubt
Whether 'tis in us to arise with day
And save ourselves unaided.

WIND AND WINDOW FLOWER

Lovers, forget your love,
    And list to the love of these,
She a window flower,
    And he a winter breeze.

When the frosty window veil   5
    Was melted down at noon,
And the cagèd yellow bird
    Hung over her in tune,

He marked her through the pane,
    He could not help but mark,   10
And only passed her by
    To come again at dark.

He was a winter wind,
    Concerned with ice and snow,

Dead weeds and unmated birds,   15
   And little of love could know.

But he sighed upon the sill,
   He gave the sash a shake,
As witness all within
   Who lay that night awake.   20

Perchance he half prevailed
   To win her for the flight
From the firelit looking-glass
   And warm stove-window light.

But the flower leaned aside   25
   And thought of naught to say,
And morning found the breeze
   A hundred miles away.

TO THE THAWING WIND

Come with rain, O loud Southwester!
Bring the singer, bring the nester;
Give the buried flower a dream;
Make the settled snowbank steam;
Find the brown beneath the white;   5
But whate'er you do tonight,
Bathe my window, make it flow,
Melt it as the ice will go;
Melt the glass and leave the sticks
Like a hermit's crucifix;   10
Burst into my narrow stall;
Swing the picture on the wall;
Run the rattling pages o'er;

11

Scatter poems on the floor;
Turn the poet out of door.   15

A PRAYER IN SPRING

Oh, give us pleasure in the flowers today;
And give us not to think so far away
As the uncertain harvest; keep us here
All simply in the springing of the year.

Oh, give us pleasure in the orchard white,   5
Like nothing else by day, like ghosts by night;
And make us happy in the happy bees,
The swarm dilating round the perfect trees.

And make us happy in the darting bird
That suddenly above the bees is heard,   10
The meteor that thrusts in with needle bill,
And off a blossom in mid-air stands still.

For this is love and nothing else is love,
The which it is reserved for God above
To sanctify to what far ends He will,   15
But which it only needs that we fulfill.

FLOWER-GATHERING

I left you in the morning,
And in the morning glow
You walked a way beside me
To make me sad to go.
Do you know me in the gloaming,   5

12

Gaunt and dusty gray with roaming?
Are you dumb because you know me not,
Or dumb because you know?

All for me? And not a question
For the faded flowers gay   10
That could take me from beside you
For the ages of a day?
They are yours, and be the measure
Of their worth for you to treasure,
The measure of the little while   15
That I've been long away.

ROSE POGONIAS

A saturated meadow,
  Sun-shaped and jewel-small,
A circle scarcely wider
  Than the trees around were tall;
Where winds were quite excluded,   5
  And the air was stifling sweet
With the breath of many flowers—
  A temple of the heat.

There we bowed us in the burning,
  As the sun's right worship is,   10
To pick where none could miss them
  A thousand orchises;
For though the grass was scattered,
  Yet every second spear
Seemed tipped with wings of color   15
  That tinged the atmosphere.

13

We raised a simple prayer
  Before we left the spot,
That in the general mowing
  That place might be forgot;   20
Or if not all so favored,
  Obtain such grace of hours
That none should mow the grass there
  While so confused with flowers.

WAITING

Afield at dusk

What things for dream there are when specter-like,
Moving among tall haycocks lightly piled,
I enter alone upon the stubble field,
From which the laborers' voices late have died,
And in the antiphony of afterglow   5
And rising full moon, sit me down
Upon the full moon's side of the first haycock
And lose myself amid so many alike.

I dream upon the opposing lights of the hour,
Preventing shadow until the moon prevail;   10
I dream upon the nighthawks peopling heaven,
Each circling each with vague unearthly cry,
Or plunging headlong with fierce twang afar;
And on the bat's mute antics, who would seem
Dimly to have made out my secret place,   15
Only to lose it when he pirouettes,
And seek it endlessly with purblind haste;
On the last swallow's sweep; and on the rasp
In the abyss of odor and rustle at my back,
That, silenced by my advent, finds once more,   20

14

After an interval, his instrument,
And tries once—twice—and thrice if I be there;
And on the worn book of old-golden song
I brought not here to read, it seems, but hold
And freshen in this air of withering sweetness;   25
But on the memory of one absent, most,
For whom these lines when they shall greet her eye.

IN A VALE

When I was young, we dwelt in a vale
   By a misty fen that rang all night,
And thus it was the maidens pale
I knew so well, whose garments trail
   Across the reeds to a window light.   5

The fen had every kind of bloom,
   And for every kind there was a face,
And a voice that has sounded in my room
Across the sill from the outer gloom.
   Each came singly unto her place,   10

But all came every night with the mist;
   And often they brought so much to say
Of things of moment to which, they wist,
One so lonely was fain to list,
   That the stars were almost faded away   15

Before the last went, heavy with dew,
   Back to the place from which she came—
Where the bird was before it flew,
Where the flower was before it grew,
   Where bird and flower were one and the same.   20

15

And thus it is I know so well
   Why the flower has odor, the bird has song.
You have only to ask me, and I can tell.
No, not vainly there did I dwell,
   Nor vainly listen all the night long.   25

A DREAM PANG

I had withdrawn in forest, and my song
Was swallowed up in leaves that blew alway;
And to the forest edge you came one day
(This was my dream) and looked and pondered long,
But did not enter, though the wish was strong: 5
You shook your pensive head as who should say,
"I dare not—too far in his footsteps stray—
He must seek me would he undo the wrong."

Not far, but near, I stood and saw it all,
Behind low boughs the trees let down outside;   10
And the sweet pang it cost me not to call
And tell you that I saw does still abide.
But 'tis not true that thus I dwelt aloof,
For the wood wakes, and you are here for proof.

IN NEGLECT

They leave us so to the way we took,
   As two in whom they were proved mistaken,
That we sit sometimes in the wayside nook,
With mischievous, vagrant, seraphic look,
   And *try* if we cannot feel forsaken.   5

16

THE VANTAGE POINT

If tired of trees I seek again mankind,
   Well I know where to hie me—in the dawn,
   To a slope where the cattle keep the lawn.
There amid lolling juniper reclined,
Myself unseen, I see in white defined   5
   Far off the homes of men, and farther still,
   The graves of men on an opposing hill,
Living or dead, whichever are to mind.

And if by noon I have too much of these,
   I have but to turn on my arm, and lo,   10
   The sunburned hillside sets my face aglow,
My breathing shakes the bluet like a breeze,
   I smell the earth, I smell the bruisèd plant,
   I look into the crater of the ant.

MOWING

There was never a sound beside the wood but one,
And that was my long scythe whispering to the ground.
What was it it whispered? I knew not well myself;
Perhaps it was something about the heat of the sun,
Something, perhaps, about the lack of sound—   5
And that was why it whispered and did not speak.
It was no dream of the gift of idle hours,
Or easy gold at the hand of fay or elf:
Anything more than the truth would have seemed too weak
To the earnest love that laid the swale in rows,   10
Not without feeble-pointed spikes of flowers
(Pale orchises), and scared a bright green snake.
The fact is the sweetest dream that labor knows.
My long scythe whispered and left the hay to make.

GOING FOR WATER

The well was dry beside the door,
   And so we went with pail and can
Across the fields behind the house
   To seek the brook if still it ran;

Not loth to have excuse to go,   5
   Because the autumn eve was fair
(Though chill), because the fields were ours,
   And by the brook our woods were there.

We ran as if to meet the moon
   That slowly dawned behind the trees,   10
The barren boughs without the leaves,
   Without the birds, without the breeze.

But once within the wood, we paused
   Like gnomes that hid us from the moon,
Ready to run to hiding new   15
   With laughter when she found us soon.

Each laid on other a staying hand
   To listen ere we dared to look,
And in the hush we joined to make
   We heard, we knew we heard the brook.   20

A note as from a single place,
   A slender tinkling fall that made
Now drops that floated on the pool
   Like pearls, and now a silver blade.

REVELATION

We make ourselves a place apart
　　Behind light words that tease and flout,
But oh, the agitated heart
　　Till someone really find us out.

'Tis pity if the case require　　　　　　　　　　5
　　(Or so we say) that in the end
We speak the literal to inspire
　　The understanding of a friend.

But so with all, from babes that play
　　At hide-and-seek to God afar,　　　　　　　10
So all who hide too well away
　　Must speak and tell us where they are.

THE TRIAL BY EXISTENCE

Even the bravest that are slain
　　Shall not dissemble their surprise
On waking to find valor reign,
　　Even as on earth, in paradise;
And where they sought without the sword　　5
　　Wide fields of asphodel fore'er,
To find that the utmost reward
　　Of daring should be still to dare.

The light of heaven falls whole and white
　　And is not shattered into dyes,　　　　　　10
The light forever is morning light;
　　The hills are verdured pasturewise;

19

The angel hosts with freshness go,
   And seek with laughter what to brave—
And binding all is the hushed snow   15
   Of the far-distant breaking wave.

And from a cliff top is proclaimed
   The gathering of the souls for birth,
The trial by existence named,
   The obscuration upon earth.   20
And the slant spirits trooping by
   In streams and cross- and counter-streams
Can but give ear to that sweet cry
   For its suggestion of what dreams!

And the more loitering are turned   25
   To view once more the sacrifice
Of those who for some good discerned
   Will gladly give up paradise.
And a white shimmering concourse rolls
   Toward the throne to witness there   30
The speeding of devoted souls
   Which God makes His especial care.

And none are taken but who will,
   Having first heard the life read out
That opens earthward, good and ill,   35
   Beyond the shadow of a doubt;
And very beautifully God limns,
   And tenderly, life's little dream,
But naught extenuates or dims,
   Setting the thing that is supreme.   40

Nor is there wanting in the press
   Some spirit to stand simply forth,

Heroic in its nakedness,
    Against the uttermost of earth.
The tale of earth's unhonored things   45
    Sounds nobler there than 'neath the sun;
And the mind whirls and the heart sings,
    And a shout greets the daring one.

But always God speaks at the end:
    "One thought in agony of strife   50
The bravest would have by for friend,
    The memory that he chose the life;
But the pure fate to which you go
    Admits no memory of choice,
Or the woe were not earthly woe   55
    To which you give the assenting voice."

And so the choice must be again,
    But the last choice is still the same;
And the awe passes wonder then,
    And a hush falls for all acclaim.   60
And God has taken a flower of gold
    And broken it, and used therefrom
The mystic link to bind and hold
    Spirit to matter till death come.

'Tis of the essence of life here,   65
    Though we choose greatly, still to lack
The lasting memory at all clear,
    That life has for us on the wrack
Nothing but what we somehow chose;
    Thus are we wholly stripped of pride   70
In the pain that has but one close,
    Bearing it crushed and mystified.

21

THE TUFT OF FLOWERS

I went to turn the grass once after one
Who mowed it in the dew before the sun.

The dew was gone that made his blade so keen
Before I came to view the leveled scene.

I looked for him behind an isle of trees;   5
I listened for his whetstone on the breeze.

But he had gone his way, the grass all mown,
And I must be, as he had been—alone,

"As all must be," I said within my heart,
"Whether they work together or apart."   10

But as I said it, swift there passed me by
On noiseless wing a bewildered butterfly,

Seeking with memories grown dim o'er night
Some resting flower of yesterday's delight.

And once I marked his flight go round and round,   15
As where some flower lay withering on the ground.

And then he flew as far as eye could see,
And then on tremulous wing came back to me.

I thought of questions that have no reply,
And would have turned to toss the grass to dry;   20

But he turned first, and led my eye to look
At a tall tuft of flowers beside a brook,

A leaping tongue of bloom the scythe had spared
Beside a reedy brook the scythe had bared.

The mower in the dew had loved them thus,   25
By leaving them to flourish, not for us,

Nor yet to draw one thought of ours to him,
But from sheer morning gladness at the brim.

The butterfly and I had lit upon,
Nevertheless, a message from the dawn,   30

That made me hear the wakening birds around,
And hear his long scythe whispering to the ground,

And feel a spirit kindred to my own;
So that henceforth I worked no more alone;

But glad with him, I worked as with his aid,   35
And weary, sought at noon with him the shade;

And dreaming, as it were, held brotherly speech
With one whose thought I had not hoped to reach.

"Men work together," I told him from the heart,
"Whether they work together or apart."   40

PAN WITH US

Pan came out of the woods one day—
His skin and his hair and his eyes were gray,
The gray of the moss of walls were they—
    And stood in the sun and looked his fill
    At wooded valley and wooded hill.   5

He stood in the zephyr, pipes in hand,
On a height of naked pasture land;
In all the country he did command

23

He saw no smoke and he saw no roof.
That was well! and he stamped a hoof.   10

His heart knew peace, for none came here
To this lean feeding, save once a year
Someone to salt the half-wild steer,
   Or homespun children with clicking pails
   Who see so little they tell no tales.   15

He tossed his pipes, too hard to teach
A new-world song, far out of reach,
For a sylvan sign that the blue jay's screech
   And the whimper of hawks beside the sun
   Were music enough for him, for one.   20

Times were changed from what they were:
Such pipes kept less of power to stir
The fruited bough of the juniper
   And the fragile bluets clustered there
   Than the merest aimless breath of air.   25

They were pipes of pagan mirth,
And the world had found new terms of worth.
He laid him down on the sunburned earth
   And raveled a flower and looked away.
   Play? Play?—What should he play?   30

THE DEMIURGE'S LAUGH

It was far in the sameness of the wood;
   I was running with joy on the Demon's trail,
Though I knew what I hunted was no true god.
   It was just as the light was beginning to fail
That I suddenly heard—all I needed to hear: 5

It has lasted me many and many a year.

The sound was behind me instead of before,
  A sleepy sound, but mocking half,
As of one who utterly couldn't care.
  The Demon arose from his wallow to laugh,   10
Brushing the dirt from his eye as he went;
And well I knew what the Demon meant.

I shall not forget how his laugh rang out.
  I felt as a fool to have been so caught,
And checked my steps to make pretense   15
  It was something among the leaves I sought
(Though doubtful whether he stayed to see).
Thereafter I sat me against a tree.

NOW CLOSE THE WINDOWS

Now close the windows and hush all the fields:
  If the trees must, let them silently toss;
No bird is singing now, and if there is,
  Be it my loss.

It will be long ere the marshes resume,   5
  It will be long ere the earliest bird:
So close the windows and not hear the wind,
  But see all wind-stirred.

IN HARDWOOD GROVES

The same leaves over and over again!
They fall from giving shade above,
To make one texture of faded brown

25

And fit the earth like a leather glove.

Before the leaves can mount again   5
To fill the trees with another shade,
They must go down past things coming up.
They must go down into the dark decayed.

They *must* be pierced by flowers and put
Beneath the feet of dancing flowers.   10
However it is in some other world
I know that this is the way in ours.

A LINE-STORM SONG

The line-storm clouds fly tattered and swift.
   The road is forlorn all day,
Where a myriad snowy quartz-stones lift,
   And the hoofprints vanish away.
The roadside flowers, too wet for the bee,   5
   Expend their bloom in vain.
Come over the hills and far with me,
   And be my love in the rain.

The birds have less to say for themselves
   In the wood-world's torn despair   10
Than now these numberless years the elves,
   Although they are no less there:
All song of the woods is crushed like some
   Wild, easily shattered rose.
Come, be my love in the wet woods, come,   15
   Where the boughs rain when it blows.

There is the gale to urge behind
   And bruit our singing down,

26

And the shallow waters aflutter with wind
   From which to gather your gown.   20
What matter if we go clear to the west,
   And come not through dry-shod?
For wilding brooch, shall wet your breast
   The rain-fresh goldenrod.

Oh, never this whelming east wind swells   25
   But it seems like the sea's return
To the ancient lands where it left the shells
   Before the age of the fern;
And it seems like the time when, after doubt,
   Our love came back amain.   30
Oh, come forth into the storm and rout
   And be my love in the rain.

OCTOBER

O hushed October morning mild,
Thy leaves have ripened to the fall;
Tomorrow's wind, if it be wild,
Should waste them all.
The crows above the forest call;   5
Tomorrow they may form and go.
O hushed October morning mild,
Begin the hours of this day slow.
Make the day seem to us less brief.
Hearts not averse to being beguiled,   10
Beguile us in the way you know.
Release one leaf at break of day;
At noon release another leaf;
One from our trees, one far away.
Retard the sun with gentle mist;   15

27

Enchant the land with amethyst.
Slow, slow!
For the grapes' sake, if they were all,
Whose leaves already are burnt with frost,
Whose clustered fruit must else be lost—   20
For the grapes' sake along the wall.

MY BUTTERFLY

Thine emulous fond flowers are dead, too,
And the daft sun-assaulter, he
That frighted thee so oft, is fled or dead:
Save only me
(Nor is it sad to thee!)—   5
Save only me
There is none left to mourn thee in the fields.

The gray grass is scarce dappled with the snow;
Its two banks have not shut upon the river;
But it is long ago—   10
It seems forever—
Since first I saw thee glance,
With all thy dazzling other ones,
In airy dalliance,
Precipitate in love,   15
Tossed, tangled, whirled and whirled above,
Like a limp rose-wreath in a fairy dance.

When that was, the soft mist
Of my regret hung not on all the land,
And I was glad for thee,   20
And glad for me, I wist.

Thou didst not know, who tottered, wandering on high,

28

That fate had made thee for the pleasure of the wind,
With those great careless wings,
Nor yet did I.   25

And there were other things:
It seemed God let thee flutter from His gentle clasp,
Then fearful He had let thee win
Too far beyond Him to be gathered in,
Snatched thee, o'ereager, with ungentle grasp.   30

Ah! I remember me
How once conspiracy was rife
Against my life—
The languor of it and the dreaming fond;
Surging, the grasses dizzied me of thought,   35
The breeze three odors brought,
And a gem-flower waved in a wand!

Then when I was distraught
And could not speak,
Sidelong, full on my cheek,   40
What should that reckless zephyr fling
But the wild touch of thy dye-dusty wing!

I found that wing broken today!
For thou art dead, I said,
And the strange birds say.   45
I found it with the withered leaves
Under the eaves.

RELUCTANCE

Out through the fields and the woods
And over the walls I have wended;

I have climbed the hills of view
    And looked at the world, and descended;
I have come by the highway home,   5
    And lo, it is ended.

The leaves are all dead on the ground,
    Save those that the oak is keeping
To ravel them one by one
    And let them go scraping and creeping   10
Out over the crusted snow,
    When others are sleeping.

And the dead leaves lie huddled and still,
    No longer blown hither and thither;
The last lone aster is gone;   15
    The flowers of the witch hazel wither;
The heart is still aching to seek,
    But the feet question "Whither?"

Ah, when to the heart of man
    Was it ever less than a treason   20
To go with the drift of things,
    To yield with a grace to reason,
And bow and accept the end
    Of a love or a season?

North of Boston

: 1914 :

MENDING WALL

Something there is that doesn't love a wall,
That sends the frozen-ground-swell under it
And spills the upper boulders in the sun,
And makes gaps even two can pass abreast.
The work of hunters is another thing: 5
I have come after them and made repair
Where they have left not one stone on a stone,
But they would have the rabbit out of hiding,
To please the yelping dogs. The gaps I mean,
No one has seen them made or heard them made,   10
But at spring mending-time we find them there.
I let my neighbor know beyond the hill;
And on a day we meet to walk the line
And set the wall between us once again.
We keep the wall between us as we go.   15
To each the boulders that have fallen to each.
And some are loaves and some so nearly balls
We have to use a spell to make them balance:
"Stay where you are until our backs are turned!"
We wear our fingers rough with handling them.   20
Oh, just another kind of outdoor game,
One on a side. It comes to little more:
There where it is we do not need the wall:
He is all pine and I am apple orchard.
My apple trees will never get across   25
And eat the cones under his pines, I tell him.
He only says, "Good fences make good neighbors."

Spring is the mischief in me, and I wonder
If I could put a notion in his head:
"*Why* do they make good neighbors? Isn't it   30
Where there are cows? But here there are no cows.
Before I built a wall I'd ask to know
What I was walling in or walling out,
And to whom I was like to give offense.
Something there is that doesn't love a wall,   35
That wants it down." I could say "Elves" to him,
But it's not elves exactly, and I'd rather
He said it for himself. I see him there,
Bringing a stone grasped firmly by the top
In each hand, like an old-stone savage armed.   40
He moves in darkness as it seems to me,
Not of woods only and the shade of trees.
He will not go behind his father's saying,
And he likes having thought of it so well
He says again, "Good fences make good neighbors."   45

THE DEATH OF THE HIRED MAN

Mary sat musing on the lamp-flame at the table,
Waiting for Warren. When she heard his step,
She ran on tiptoe down the darkened passage
To meet him in the doorway with the news
And put him on his guard. "Silas is back."   5
She pushed him outward with her through the door
And shut it after her. "Be kind," she said.
She took the market things from Warren's arms
And set them on the porch, then drew him down
To sit beside her on the wooden steps.   10

"When was I ever anything but kind to him?

34

But I'll not have the fellow back," he said.
"I told him so last haying, didn't I?
If he left then, I said, that ended it.
What good is he? Who else will harbor him   15
At his age for the little he can do?
What help he is there's no depending on.
Off he goes always when I need him most.
He thinks he ought to earn a little pay,
Enough at least to buy tobacco with,   20
So he won't have to beg and be beholden.
'All right,' I say, 'I can't afford to pay
Any fixed wages, though I wish I could.'
'Someone else can.' 'Then someone else will have to.'
I shouldn't mind his bettering himself   25
If that was what it was. You can be certain,
When he begins like that, there's someone at him
Trying to coax him off with pocket money—
In haying time, when any help is scarce.
In winter he comes back to us. I'm done."   30

"Sh! not so loud: he'll hear you," Mary said.

"I want him to: he'll have to soon or late."

"He's worn out. He's asleep beside the stove.
When I came up from Rowe's I found him here,
Huddled against the barn door fast asleep,   35
A miserable sight, and frightening, too—
You needn't smile—I didn't recognize him—
I wasn't looking for him—and he's changed.
Wait till you see."

                "Where did you say he'd been?"

"He didn't say. I dragged him to the house,   40

35

And gave him tea and tried to make him smoke.
I tried to make him talk about his travels.
Nothing would do: he just kept nodding off."

"What did he say? Did he say anything?"

"But little."

    "Anything? Mary, confess   45
He said he'd come to ditch the meadow for me."

"Warren!"

    "But did he? I just want to know."

"Of course he did. What would you have him say?
Surely you wouldn't grudge the poor old man
Some humble way to save his self-respect.   50
He added, if you really care to know,
He meant to clear the upper pasture, too.
That sounds like something you have heard before?
Warren, I wish you could have heard the way
He jumbled everything. I stopped to look   55
Two or three times—he made me feel so queer—
To see if he was talking in his sleep.
He ran on Harold Wilson—you remember—
The boy you had in haying four years since.
He's finished school, and teaching in his college.   60
Silas declares you'll have to get him back.
He says they two will make a team for work:
Between them they will lay this farm as smooth!
The way he mixed that in with other things.
He thinks young Wilson a likely lad, though daft   65
On education—you know how they fought
All through July under the blazing sun,
Silas up on the cart to build the load,

36

Harold along beside to pitch it on."

"Yes, I took care to keep well out of earshot."   70

"Well, those days trouble Silas like a dream.
You wouldn't think they would. How some things linger!
Harold's young college-boy's assurance piqued him.
After so many years he still keeps finding
Good arguments he sees he might have used.   75
I sympathize. I know just how it feels
To think of the right thing to say too late.
Harold's associated in his mind with Latin.
He asked me what I thought of Harold's saying
He studied Latin, like the violin,   80
Because he liked it—that an argument!
He said he couldn't make the boy believe
He could find water with a hazel prong—
Which showed how much good school had ever done him.
He wanted to go over that. But most of all   85
He thinks if he could have another chance
To teach him how to build a load of hay——"

"I know, that's Silas' one accomplishment.
He bundles every forkful in its place,
And tags and numbers it for future reference,   90
So he can find and easily dislodge it
In the unloading. Silas does that well.
He takes it out in bunches like big birds' nests.
You never see him standing on the hay
He's trying to lift, straining to lift himself."   95

"He thinks if he could teach him that, he'd be
Some good perhaps to someone in the world.
He hates to see a boy the fool of books.
Poor Silas, so concerned for other folk,

And nothing to look backward to with pride,   100
And nothing to look forward to with hope,
So now and never any different."

Part of a moon was falling down the west,
Dragging the whole sky with it to the hills.
Its light poured softly in her lap. She saw it   105
And spread her apron to it. She put out her hand
Among the harplike morning-glory strings,
Taut with the dew from garden bed to eaves,
As if she played unheard some tenderness
That wrought on him beside her in the night.   110
"Warren," she said, "he has come home to die:
You needn't be afraid he'll leave you this time."

"Home," he mocked gently.

                          "Yes, what else but home?
It all depends on what you mean by home.
Of course he's nothing to us, any more   115
Than was the hound that came a stranger to us
Out of the woods, worn out upon the trail."

"Home is the place where, when you have to go there,
They have to take you in."

                          "I should have called it
Something you somehow haven't to deserve."   120

Warren leaned out and took a step or two,
Picked up a little stick, and brought it back
And broke it in his hand and tossed it by.
"Silas has better claim on us you think
Than on his brother? Thirteen little miles   125
As the road winds would bring him to his door.
Silas has walked that far no doubt today.

38

Why doesn't he go there? His brother's rich,
A somebody—director in the bank."

"He never told us that."

                              "We know it, though."   130

"I think his brother ought to help, of course.
I'll see to that if there is need. He ought of right
To take him in, and might be willing to—
He may be better than appearances.
But have some pity on Silas. Do you think   135
If he had any pride in claiming kin
Or anything he looked for from his brother,
He'd keep so still about him all this time?"

"I wonder what's between them."

                              "I can tell you.
Silas is what he is—we wouldn't mind him—   140
But just the kind that kinsfolk can't abide.
He never did a thing so very bad.
He don't know why he isn't quite as good
As anybody. Worthless though he is,
He won't be made ashamed to please his brother."   145

"*I* can't think Si ever hurt anyone."

"No, but he hurt my heart the way he lay
And rolled his old head on that sharp-edged chair-back.
He wouldn't let me put him on the lounge.
You must go in and see what you can do.   150
I made the bed up for him there tonight.
You'll be surprised at him—how much he's broken.
His working days are done; I'm sure of it."

"I'd not be in a hurry to say that."

"I haven't been. Go, look, see for yourself.   155
But, Warren, please remember how it is:
He's come to help you ditch the meadow.
He has a plan. You mustn't laugh at him.
He may not speak of it, and then he may.
I'll sit and see if that small sailing cloud   160
Will hit or miss the moon."

             It hit the moon.
Then there were three there, making a dim row,
The moon, the little silver cloud, and she.

Warren returned—too soon, it seemed to her—
Slipped to her side, caught up her hand and waited.   165

"Warren?" she questioned.

            "Dead," was all he answered.

THE MOUNTAIN

The mountain held the town as in a shadow.
I saw so much before I slept there once:
I noticed that I missed stars in the west,
Where its black body cut into the sky.
Near me it seemed: I felt it like a wall   5
Behind which I was sheltered from a wind.
And yet between the town and it I found,
When I walked forth at dawn to see new things,
Were fields, a river, and beyond, more fields.
The river at the time was fallen away,   10
And made a widespread brawl on cobblestones;
But the signs showed what it had done in spring:
Good grassland gullied out, and in the grass
Ridges of sand, and driftwood stripped of bark.

I crossed the river and swung round the mountain.　　15
And there I met a man who moved so slow
With white-faced oxen, in a heavy cart,
It seemed no harm to stop him altogether.

"What town is this?" I asked.

　　　　　　　　"This? Lunenburg."

Then I was wrong: the town of my sojourn,　　20
Beyond the bridge, was not that of the mountain,
But only felt at night its shadowy presence.
"Where is your village? Very far from here?"

"There is no village—only scattered farms.
We were but sixty voters last election.　　25
We can't in nature grow to many more:
That thing takes all the room!" He moved his goad.
The mountain stood there to be pointed at.
Pasture ran up the side a little way,
And then there was a wall of trees with trunks;　　30
After that only tops of trees, and cliffs
Imperfectly concealed among the leaves.
A dry ravine emerged from under boughs
Into the pasture.

　　　　　　"That looks like a path.
Is that the way to reach the top from here?—　　35
Not for this morning, but some other time:
I must be getting back to breakfast now."

"I don't advise your trying from this side.
There is no proper path, but those that *have*
Been up, I understand, have climbed from Ladd's.　　40
That's five miles back. You can't mistake the place:
They logged it there last winter some way up.

41

I'd take you, but I'm bound the other way."

"You've never climbed it?"

                       "I've been on the sides,
Deer-hunting and trout-fishing. There's a brook   45
That starts up on it somewhere—I've heard say
Right on the top, tip-top—a curious thing.
But what would interest you about the brook,
It's always cold in summer, warm in winter.
One of the great sights going is to see   50
It steam in winter like an ox's breath,
Until the bushes all along its banks
Are inch-deep with the frosty spines and bristles—
You know the kind. Then let the sun shine on it!"

"There ought to be a view around the world   55
From such a mountain—if it isn't wooded
Clear to the top." I saw through leafy screens
Great granite terraces in sun and shadow,
Shelves one could rest a knee on getting up—
With depths behind him sheer a hundred feet—   60
Or turn and sit on and look out and down,
With little ferns in crevices at his elbow.

"As to that I can't say. But there's the spring,
Right on the summit, almost like a fountain.
That ought to be worth seeing."

                       "If it's there.   65
You never saw it?"

                "I guess there's no doubt
About its being there. I never saw it.
It may not be right on the very top:
It wouldn't have to be a long way down

To have some head of water from above,   70
And a *good distance* down might not be noticed
By anyone who'd come a long way up.
One time I asked a fellow climbing it
To look and tell me later how it was."

"What did he say?"

                                        "He said there was a lake   75
Somewhere in Ireland on a mountain top."

"But a lake's different. What about the spring?"

"He never got up high enough to see.
That's why I don't advise your trying this side.
He tried this side. I've always meant to go   80
And look myself, but you know how it is:
It doesn't seem so much to climb a mountain
You've worked around the foot of all your life.
What would I do? Go in my overalls,
With a big stick, the same as when the cows   85
Haven't come down to the bars at milking time?
Or with a shotgun for a stray black bear?
'Twouldn't seem real to climb for climbing it."

"I shouldn't climb it if I didn't want to—
Not for the sake of climbing. What's its name?"   90

"We call it Hor: I don't know if that's right."

"Can one walk around it? Would it be too far?"

"You can drive round and keep in Lunenburg,
But it's as much as ever you can do,
The boundary lines keep in so close to it.   95
Hor is the township, and the township's Hor—
And a few houses sprinkled round the foot,

43

Like boulders broken off the upper cliff,
Rolled out a little farther than the rest."

"Warm in December, cold in June, you say?" 100

"I don't suppose the water's changed at all.
You and I know enough to know it's warm
Compared with cold, and cold compared with warm.
But all the fun's in how you say a thing."

"You've lived here all your life?"

                     "Ever since Hor 105
Was no bigger than a———" What, I did not hear.
He drew the oxen toward him with light touches
Of his slim goad on nose and offside flank,
Gave them their marching orders and was moving.

A HUNDRED COLLARS

Lancaster bore him—such a little town,
Such a great man. It doesn't see him often
Of late years, though he keeps the old homestead
And sends the children down there with their mother
To run wild in the summer—a little wild. 5
Sometimes he joins them for a day or two
And sees old friends he somehow can't get near.
They meet him in the general store at night,
Preoccupied with formidable mail,
Rifling a printed letter as he talks. 10
They seem afraid. He wouldn't have it so:
Though a great scholar, he's a democrat,
If not at heart, at least on principle.

Lately when coming up to Lancaster,
His train being late, he missed another train 15

44

And had four hours to wait at Woodsville Junction
After eleven o'clock at night. Too tired
To think of sitting such an ordeal out,
He turned to the hotel to find a bed.

"No room," the night clerk said. "Unless——"   20

Woodsville's a place of shrieks and wandering lamps
And cars that shock and rattle—and *one* hotel.

"You say 'unless.'"

                    "Unless you wouldn't mind
Sharing a room with someone else."

                              "Who is it?"

"A man."

          "So I should hope. What kind of man?"   25

"I know him: he's all right. A man's a man.
Separate beds, of course, you understand."
The night clerk blinked his eyes and dared him on.

"Who's that man sleeping in the office chair?
Has he had the refusal of my chance?"   30

"He was afraid of being robbed or murdered.
What do you say?"

                    "I'll have to have a bed."

The night clerk led him up three flights of stairs
And down a narrow passage full of doors,
At the last one of which he knocked and entered.   35
"Lafe, here's a fellow wants to share your room."

"Show him this way. I'm not afraid of him.
I'm not so drunk I can't take care of myself."

45

The night clerk clapped a bedstead on the foot.
"This will be yours. Good-night," he said, and went.   40

"Lafe was the name, I think?"

                              "Yes, *Lay*fayette.
You got it the first time. And yours?"

                                   "Magoon.
Doctor Magoon."

                "A Doctor?"

                              "Well, a teacher."

"Professor Square-the-circle-till-you're-tired?
Hold on, there's something I don't think of now   45
That I had on my mind to ask the first
Man that knew anything I happened in with.
I'll ask you later—don't let me forget it."

The Doctor looked at Lafe and looked away.
A man? A brute. Naked above the waist,   50
He sat there creased and shining in the light,
Fumbling the buttons in a well-starched shirt.
"I'm moving into a size-larger shirt.
I've felt mean lately; mean's no name for it.
I just found what the matter was tonight: 55
I've been a-choking like a nursery tree
When it outgrows the wire band of its name tag.
I blamed it on the hot spell we've been having.
'Twas nothing but my foolish hanging back,
Not liking to own up I'd grown a size.   60
Number eighteen this is. What size do you wear?"

The Doctor caught his throat convulsively.
"Oh—ah—fourteen—fourteen."

46

               "Fourteen! You say so!
I can remember when I wore fourteen.
And come to think I must have back at home   65
More than a hundred collars, size fourteen.
Too bad to waste them all. You ought to have them.
They're yours and welcome; let me send them to you.—
What makes you stand there on one leg like that?
You're not much furtherer than where Kike left you.   70
You act as if you wished you hadn't come.
Sit down or lie down, friend; you make me nervous."

The Doctor made a subdued dash for it,
And propped himself at bay against a pillow.

"Not that way, with your shoes on Kike's white bed.   75
You can't rest that way. Let me pull your shoes off."

"Don't touch me, please—I say, don't touch me, please.
I'll not be put to bed by you, my man."

"Just as you say. Have it your own way, then.
'My man' is it? You talk like a professor.   80
Speaking of who's afraid of who, however,
I'm thinking I have more to lose than you
If anything should happen to be wrong.
Who wants to cut your number fourteen throat!
Let's have a showdown as an evidence   85
Of good faith. There is ninety dollars.
Come, if you're not afraid."

                 "I'm not afraid.
There's five: that's all I carry."

                     "I can search you?
Where are you moving over to? Stay still.
You'd better tuck your money under you   90

And sleep on it, the way I always do
When I'm with people I don't trust at night."

"Will you believe me if I put it there
Right on the counterpane—that I do trust you?"

"You'd say so, Mister Man.—I'm a collector.   95
My ninety isn't mine—you won't think that.
I pick it up a dollar at a time
All round the country for the *Weekly News*,
Published in Bow. You know the *Weekly News*?"

"Known it since I was young."

                              "Then you know me.   100
Now we are getting on together—talking.
I'm sort of Something for it at the front.
My business is to find what people want:
They pay for it, and so they ought to have it.
Fairbanks, he says to me—he's editor—   105
'Feel out the public sentiment'—he says.
A good deal comes on me when all is said.
The only trouble is we disagree
In politics: I'm Vermont Democrat—
You know what that is, sort of double-dyed;   110
The *News* has always been Republican.
Fairbanks, he says to me, 'Help us this year,'
Meaning by us their ticket. 'No,' I says,
'I can't and won't. You've been in long enough:
It's time you turned around and boosted us.   115
You'll have to pay me more than ten a week
If I'm expected to elect Bill Taft.
I doubt if I could do it anyway.' "

"You seem to shape the paper's policy."

"You see I'm in with everybody, know 'em all.   120
I almost know their farms as well as they do."

"You drive around? It must be pleasant work."

"It's business, but I can't say it's not fun.
What I like best's the lay of different farms,
Coming out on them from a stretch of woods,   125
Or over a hill or round a sudden corner.
I like to find folks getting out in spring,
Raking the dooryard, working near the house.
Later they get out further in the fields.
Everything's shut sometimes except the barn;   130
The family's all away in some back meadow.
There's a hay load a-coming—when it comes.
And later still they all get driven in:
The fields are stripped to lawn, the garden patches
Stripped to bare ground, the maple trees   135
To whips and poles. There's nobody about.
The chimney, though, keeps up a good brisk smoking.
And I lie back and ride. I take the reins
Only when someone's coming, and the mare
Stops when she likes: I tell her when to go.   140
I've spoiled Jemima in more ways than one.
She's got so she turns in at every house
As if she had some sort of curvature,
No matter if I have no errand there.
She thinks I'm sociable. I maybe am.   145
It's seldom I get down except for meals, though.
Folks entertain me from the kitchen doorstep,
All in a family row down to the youngest."

"One would suppose they might not be as glad
To see you as you are to see them."

49

Because I want their dollar? I don't want
Anything they've not got. I never dun.
I'm there, and they can pay me if they like.
I go nowhere on purpose: I happen by.—
Sorry there is no cup to give you a drink.   155
I drink out of the bottle—not your style.
Mayn't I offer you——?"

                    "No, no, no, thank you."

"Just as you say. Here's looking at you, then.—
And now I'm leaving you a little while.
You'll rest easier when I'm gone, perhaps—   160
Lie down—let yourself go and get some sleep.
But first—let's see—what was I going to ask you?
Those collars—who shall I address them to,
Suppose you aren't awake when I come back?"

"Really, friend, I can't let you. You—may need them." 165

"Not till I shrink, when they'll be out of style."

"But really I—I have so many collars."

"I don't know who I rather would have have them.
They're only turning yellow where they are.
But you're the doctor, as the saying is.   170
I'll put the light out. Don't you wait for me:
I've just begun the night. You get some sleep.
I'll knock so-fashion and peep round the door
When I come back, so you'll know who it is.
There's nothing I'm afraid of like scared people.   175
I don't want you should shoot me in the head.—
What am I doing carrying off this bottle?—
There now, you get some sleep."

He shut the door.
The Doctor slid a little down the pillow.

HOME BURIAL

He saw her from the bottom of the stairs
Before she saw him. She was starting down,
Looking back over her shoulder at some fear.
She took a doubtful step and then undid it
To raise herself and look again. He spoke   5
Advancing toward her: "What is it you see
From up there always?—for I want to know."
She turned and sank upon her skirts at that,
And her face changed from terrified to dull.
He said to gain time: "What is it you see?"   10
Mounting until she cowered under him.
"I will find out now—you must tell me, dear."
She, in her place, refused him any help,
With the least stiffening of her neck and silence.
She let him look, sure that he wouldn't see,   15
Blind creature; and awhile he didn't see.
But at last he murmured, "Oh," and again, "Oh."

"What is it—what?" she said.

                    "Just that I see."

"You don't," she challenged. "Tell me what it is."

"The wonder is I didn't see at once.   20
I never noticed it from here before.
I must be wonted to it—that's the reason.
The little graveyard where my people are!
So small the window frames the whole of it.
Not so much larger than a bedroom, is it?   25

51

There are three stones of slate and one of marble,
Broad-shouldered little slabs there in the sunlight
On the sidehill. We haven't to mind *those*.
But I understand: it is not the stones,
But the child's mound——"

                                 "Don't, don't, don't,
  don't," she cried.   30

She withdrew, shrinking from beneath his arm
That rested on the banister, and slid downstairs;
And turned on him with such a daunting look,
He said twice over before he knew himself:
"Can't a man speak of his own child he's lost?"   35

"Not you!—Oh, where's my hat? Oh, I don't need it!
I must get out of here. I must get air.—
I don't know rightly whether any man can."

"Amy! Don't go to someone else this time.
Listen to me. I won't come down the stairs."   40
He sat and fixed his chin between his fists.
"There's something I should like to ask you, dear."

"You don't know how to ask it."

                                 "Help me, then."

Her fingers moved the latch for all reply.

"My words are nearly always an offense.   45
I don't know how to speak of anything
So as to please you. But I might be taught,
I should suppose. I can't say I see how.
A man must partly give up being a man
With womenfolk. We could have some arrangement 50
By which I'd bind myself to keep hands off

52

Anything special you're a-mind to name.
Though I don't like such things 'twixt those that love.
Two that don't love can't live together without them.
But two that do can't live together with them."   55
She moved the latch a little. "Don't—don't go.
Don't carry it to someone else this time.
Tell me about it if it's something human.
Let me into your grief. I'm not so much
Unlike other folks as your standing there   60
Apart would make me out. Give me my chance.
I do think, though, you overdo it a little.
What was it brought you up to think it the thing
To take your mother-loss of a first child
So inconsolably—in the face of love.   65
You'd think his memory might be satisfied——"

"There you go sneering now!"

                        "I'm not, I'm not!
You make me angry. I'll come down to you.
God, what a woman! And it's come to this,
A man can't speak of his own child that's dead."   70

"You can't because you don't know how to speak.
If you had any feelings, you that dug
With your own hand—how could you?—his little grave;
I saw you from that very window there,
Making the gravel leap and leap in air,   75
Leap up, like that, like that, and land so lightly
And roll back down the mound beside the hole.
I thought, Who is that man? I didn't know you.
And I crept down the stairs and up the stairs
To look again, and still your spade kept lifting.   80
Then you came in. I heard your rumbling voice

53

Out in the kitchen, and I don't know why,
But I went near to see with my own eyes.
You could sit there with the stains on your shoes
Of the fresh earth from your own baby's grave   85
And talk about your everyday concerns.
You had stood the spade up against the wall
Outside there in the entry, for I saw it."

"I shall laugh the worst laugh I ever laughed.
I'm cursed. God, if I don't believe I'm cursed."   90

"I can repeat the very words you were saying:
'Three foggy mornings and one rainy day
Will rot the best birch fence a man can build.'
Think of it, talk like that at such a time!
What had how long it takes a birch to rot   95
To do with what was in the darkened parlor?
You *couldn't* care! The nearest friends can go
With anyone to death, comes so far short
They might as well not try to go at all.
No, from the time when one is sick to death,   100
One is alone, and he dies more alone.
Friends make pretense of following to the grave,
But before one is in it, their minds are turned
And making the best of their way back to life
And living people, and things they understand.   105
But the world's evil. I won't have grief so
If I can change it. Oh, I won't, I won't!"

"There, you have said it all and you feel better.
You won't go now. You're crying. Close the door.
The heart's gone out of it: why keep it up?   110
Amy! There's someone coming down the road!"

"*You*—oh, you think the talk is all. I must go—

54

Somewhere out of this house. How can I make you——"

"If—you—do!" She was opening the door wider.
"Where do you mean to go? First tell me that.   115
I'll follow and bring you back by force. I *will!*—"

THE BLACK COTTAGE

We chanced in passing by that afternoon
To catch it in a sort of special picture
Among tar-banded ancient cherry trees,
Set well back from the road in rank lodged grass,
The little cottage we were speaking of,   5
A front with just a door between two windows,
Fresh painted by the shower a velvet black.
We paused, the minister and I, to look.
He made as if to hold it at arm's length
Or put the leaves aside that framed it in.   10
"Pretty," he said. "Come in. No one will care."
The path was a vague parting in the grass
That led us to a weathered windowsill.
We pressed our faces to the pane. "You see," he said,
"Everything's as she left it when she died.   15
Her sons won't sell the house or the things in it.
They say they mean to come and summer here
Where they were boys. They haven't come this year.
They live so far away—one is out West—
It will be hard for them to keep their word.   20
Anyway they won't have the place disturbed."
A buttoned haircloth lounge spread scrolling arms
Under a crayon portrait on the wall,
Done sadly from an old daguerreotype.
"That was the father as he went to war.   25

55

She always, when she talked about the war,
Sooner or later came and leaned, half knelt,
Against the lounge beside it, though I doubt
If such unlifelike lines kept power to stir
Anything in her after all the years. 30
He fell at Gettysburg or Fredericksburg,
I ought to know—it makes a difference which:
Fredericksburg wasn't Gettysburg, of course.
But what I'm getting to is how forsaken
A little cottage this has always seemed; 35
Since she went, more than ever, but before—
I don't mean altogether by the lives
That had gone out of it, the father first,
Then the two sons, till she was left alone.
(Nothing could draw her after those two sons. 40
She valued the considerate neglect
She had at some cost taught them after years.)
I mean by the world's having passed it by—
As we almost got by this afternoon.
It always seems to me a sort of mark 45
To measure how far fifty years have brought us.
Why not sit down if you are in no haste?
These doorsteps seldom have a visitor.
The warping boards pull out their own old nails
With none to tread and put them in their place. 50
She had her own idea of things, the old lady.
And she liked talk. She had seen Garrison
And Whittier, and had her story of them.
One wasn't long in learning that she thought,
Whatever else the Civil War was for, 55
It wasn't just to keep the States together,
Nor just to free the slaves, though it did both.
She wouldn't have believed those ends enough

To have given outright for them all she gave.
Her giving somehow touched the principle   60
That all men are created free and equal.
And to hear her quaint phrases—so removed
From the world's view today of all those things.
That's a hard mystery of Jefferson's.
What did he mean? Of course the easy way   65
Is to decide it simply isn't true.
It may not be. I heard a fellow say so.
But never mind, the Welshman got it planted
Where it will trouble us a thousand years.
Each age will have to reconsider it.   70
You couldn't tell her what the West was saying,
And what the South, to her serene belief.
She had some art of hearing and yet not
Hearing the latter wisdom of the world.
White was the only race she ever knew.   75
Black she had scarcely seen, and yellow never.
But how could they be made so very unlike
By the same hand working in the same stuff?
She had supposed the war decided that.
What are you going to do with such a person?   80
Strange how such innocence gets its own way.
I shouldn't be surprised if in this world
It were the force that would at last prevail.
Do you know but for her there was a time
When, to please younger members of the church, 85
Or rather say non-members in the church,
Whom we all have to think of nowadays,
I would have changed the Creed a very little?
Not that she ever had to ask me not to;
It never got so far as that; but the bare thought   90
Of her old tremulous bonnet in the pew,

57

And of her half asleep, was too much for me.
Why, I might wake her up and startle her.
It was the words 'descended into Hades'
That seemed too pagan to our liberal youth.   95
You know they suffered from a general onslaught.
And well, if they weren't true why keep right on
Saying them like the heathen? We could drop them.
Only—there was the bonnet in the pew.
Such a phrase couldn't have meant much to her.   100
But suppose she had missed it from the Creed,
As a child misses the unsaid Good-night
And falls asleep with heartache—how should *I* feel?
I'm just as glad she made me keep hands off,
For, dear me, why abandon a belief   105
Merely because it ceases to be true.
Cling to it long enough, and not a doubt
It will turn true again, for so it goes.
Most of the change we think we see in life
Is due to truths being in and out of favor.   110
As I sit here, and oftentimes, I wish
I could be monarch of a desert land
I could devote and dedicate forever
To the truths we keep coming back and back to.
So desert it would have to be, so walled   115
By mountain ranges half in summer snow,
No one would covet it or think it worth
The pains of conquering to force change on.
Scattered oases where men dwelt, but mostly
Sand dunes held loosely in tamarisk   120
Blown over and over themselves in idleness.
Sand grains should sugar in the natal dew
The babe born to the desert, the sandstorm

58

Retard mid-waste my cowering caravans—

"There are bees in this wall." He struck the clapboards, 125
Fierce heads looked out; small bodies pivoted.
We rose to go. Sunset blazed on the windows.

BLUEBERRIES

"You ought to have seen what I saw on my way
To the village, through Patterson's pasture today:
Blueberries as big as the end of your thumb,
Real sky-blue, and heavy, and ready to drum
In the cavernous pail of the first one to come!   5
And all ripe together, not some of them green
And some of them ripe! You ought to have seen!"

"I don't know what part of the pasture you mean."

"You know where they cut off the woods—let me see—
It was two years ago—or no!—can it be   10
No longer than that?—and the following fall
The fire ran and burned it all up but the wall."

"Why, there hasn't been time for the bushes to grow.
That's always the way with the blueberries, though:
There may not have been the ghost of a sign   15
Of them anywhere under the shade of the pine,
But get the pine out of the way, you may burn
The pasture all over until not a fern
Or grass-blade is left, not to mention a stick,
And presto, they're up all around you as thick   20
And hard to explain as a conjuror's trick."

"It must be on charcoal they fatten their fruit.
I taste in them sometimes the flavor of soot.

And after all, really they're ebony skinned:
The blue's but a mist from the breath of the wind, 25
A tarnish that goes at a touch of the hand,
And less than the tan with which pickers are tanned."

"Does Patterson know what he has, do you think?"

"He may and not care, and so leave the chewink
To gather them for him—you know what he is. 30
He won't make the fact that they're rightfully his
An excuse for keeping us other folk out."

"I wonder you didn't see Loren about."

"The best of it was that I did. Do you know,
I was just getting through what the field had to show 35
And over the wall and into the road,
When who should come by, with a democrat-load
Of all the young chattering Lorens alive,
But Loren, the fatherly, out for a drive."

"He saw you, then? What did he do? Did he frown?" 40

"He just kept nodding his head up and down.
You know how politely he always goes by.
But he thought a big thought—I could tell by his eye—
Which being expressed, might be this in effect:
'I have left those there berries, I shrewdly suspect, 45
To ripen too long. I am greatly to blame.'"

"He's a thriftier person than some I could name."

"He seems to be thrifty; and hasn't he need,
With the mouths of all those young Lorens to feed?
He has brought them all up on wild berries, they say, 50
Like birds. They store a great many away.
They eat them the year round, and those they don't eat

60

They sell in the store and buy shoes for their feet."

"Who cares what they say? It's a nice way to live,
Just taking what Nature is willing to give,   55
Not forcing her hand with harrow and plow."

"I wish you had seen his perpetual bow—
And the air of the youngsters! Not one of them turned,
And they looked so solemn-absurdly concerned."

"I wish I knew half what the flock of them know   60
Of where all the berries and other things grow,
Cranberries in bogs and raspberries on top
Of the boulder-strewn mountain, and when they will crop.
I met them one day and each had a flower
Stuck into his berries as fresh as a shower;   65
Some strange kind—they told me it hadn't a name."

"I've told you how once, not long after we came,
I almost provoked poor Loren to mirth
By going to him of all people on earth
To ask if he knew any fruit to be had   70
For the picking. The rascal, he said he'd be glad
To tell if he knew. But the year had been bad.
There *had* been some berries—but those were all gone.
He didn't say where they had been. He went on:
'I'm sure—I'm sure'—as polite as could be.   75
He spoke to his wife in the door, 'Let me see,
Mame, *we* don't know any good berrying place?'
It was all he could do to keep a straight face."

"If he thinks all the fruit that grows wild is for him,
He'll find he's mistaken. See here, for a whim,   80
We'll pick in the Pattersons' pasture this year.
We'll go in the morning, that is, if it's clear,

61

And the sun shines out warm: the vines must be wet.
It's so long since I picked I almost forget
How we used to pick berries: we took one look round,   85
Then sank out of sight like trolls underground,
And saw nothing more of each other, or heard,
Unless when you said I was keeping a bird
Away from its nest, and I said it was you.
'Well, one of us is.' For complaining it flew   90
Around and around us. And then for a while
We picked, till I feared you had wandered a mile,
And I thought I had lost you. I lifted a shout
Too loud for the distance you were, it turned out,
For when you made answer, your voice was as low   95
As talking—you stood up beside me, you know."

"We shan't have the place to ourselves to enjoy—
Not likely, when all the young Lorens deploy.
They'll be there tomorrow, or even tonight.
They won't be too friendly—they may be polite—   100
To people they look on as having no right
To pick where they're picking. But we won't complain.
You ought to have seen how it looked in the rain,
The fruit mixed with water in layers of leaves,
Like two kinds of jewels, a vision for thieves."   105

A SERVANT TO SERVANTS

I didn't make you know how glad I was
To have you come and camp here on our land.
I promised myself to get down some day
And see the way you lived, but I don't know!
With a houseful of hungry men to feed   5
I guess you'd find. . . . It seems to me

I can't express my feelings, any more
Than I can raise my voice or want to lift
My hand (oh, I can lift it when I have to).
Did ever you feel so? I hope you never. 10
It's got so I don't even know for sure
Whether I *am* glad, sorry, or anything.
There's nothing but a voice-like left inside
That seems to tell me how I ought to feel,
And would feel if I wasn't all gone wrong. 15
You take the lake. I look and look at it.
I see it's a fair, pretty sheet of water.
I stand and make myself repeat out loud
The advantages it has, so long and narrow,
Like a deep piece of some old running river 20
Cut short off at both ends. It lies five miles
Straightaway through the mountain notch
From the sink window where I wash the plates,
And all our storms come up toward the house,
Drawing the slow waves whiter and whiter and whiter. 25
It took my mind off doughnuts and soda biscuit
To step outdoors and take the water dazzle
A sunny morning, or take the rising wind
About my face and body and through my wrapper,
When a storm threatened from the Dragon's Den, 30
And a cold chill shivered across the lake.
I see it's a fair, pretty sheet of water,
Our Willoughby! How did you hear of it?
I expect, though, everyone's heard of it.
In a book about ferns? Listen to that! 35
You let things more like feathers regulate
Your going and coming. And you like it here?
I can see how you might. But I don't know!
It would be different if more people came,

For then there would be business. As it is,   40
The cottages Len built, sometimes we rent them,
Sometimes we don't. We've a good piece of shore
That ought to be worth something, and may yet.
But I don't count on it as much as Len.
He looks on the bright side of everything,   45
Including me. He thinks I'll be all right
With doctoring. But it's not medicine—
Lowe is the only doctor's dared to say so—
It's rest I want—there, I have said it out—
From cooking meals for hungry hired men   50
And washing dishes after them—from doing
Things over and over that just won't stay done.
By good rights I ought not to have so much
Put on me, but there seems no other way.
Len says one steady pull more ought to do it.   55
He says the best way out is always through.
And I agree to that, or in so far
As that I can see no way out but through—
Leastways for me—and then they'll be convinced.
It's not that Len don't want the best for me.   60
It was his plan our moving over in
Beside the lake from where that day I showed you
We used to live—ten miles from anywhere.
We didn't change without some sacrifice,
But Len went at it to make up the loss.   65
His work's a man's, of course, from sun to sun,
But he works when he works as hard as I do—
Though there's small profit in comparisons.
(Women and men will make them all the same.)
But work ain't all. Len undertakes too much.   70
He's into everything in town. This year
It's highways, and he's got too many men

64

Around him to look after that make waste.
They take advantage of him shamefully,
And proud, too, of themselves for doing so.   75
We have four here to board, great good-for-nothings,
Sprawling about the kitchen with their talk
While I fry their bacon. Much they care!
No more put out in what they do or say
Than if I wasn't in the room at all.   80
Coming and going all the time, they are:
I don't learn what their names are, let alone
Their characters, or whether they are safe
To have inside the house with doors unlocked.
I'm not afraid of them, though, if they're not   85
Afraid of me. There's two can play at that.
I have my fancies: it runs in the family.
My father's brother wasn't right. They kept him
Locked up for years back there at the old farm.
I've been away once—yes, I've been away.   90
The State Asylum. I was prejudiced;
I wouldn't have sent anyone of mine there;
You know the old idea—the only asylum
Was the poorhouse, and those who could afford,
Rather than send their folks to such a place,   95
Kept them at home; and it does seem more human.
But it's not so: the place is the asylum.
There they have every means proper to do with,
And you aren't darkening other people's lives—
Worse than no good to them, and they no good   100
To you in your condition; you can't know
Affection or the want of it in that state.
I've heard too much of the old-fashioned way.
My father's brother, he went mad quite young.
Some thought he had been bitten by a dog,   105

65

Because his violence took on the form
Of carrying his pillow in his teeth;
But it's more likely he was crossed in love,
Or so the story goes. It was some girl.
Anyway all he talked about was love.   110
They soon saw he would do someone a mischief
If he wa'n't kept strict watch of, and it ended
In father's building him a sort of cage,
Or room within a room, of hickory poles,
Like stanchions in the barn, from floor to ceiling—   115
A narrow passage all the way around.
Anything they put in for furniture
He'd tear to pieces, even a bed to lie on.
So they made the place comfortable with straw,
Like a beast's stall, to ease their consciences.   120
Of course they had to feed him without dishes.
They tried to keep him clothed, but he paraded
With his clothes on his arm—all of his clothes.
Cruel—it sounds. I s'pose they did the best
They knew. And just when he was at the height,   125
Father and mother married, and mother came,
A bride, to help take care of such a creature,
And accommodate her young life to his.
That was what marrying father meant to her.
She had to lie and hear love things made dreadful   130
By his shouts in the night. He'd shout and shout
Until the strength was shouted out of him,
And his voice died down slowly from exhaustion.
He'd pull his bars apart like bow and bowstring,
And let them go and make them twang, until   135
His hands had worn them smooth as any oxbow.
And then he'd crow as if he thought that child's play—
The only fun he had. I've heard them say, though,

They found a way to put a stop to it.
He was before my time—I never saw him;   140
But the pen stayed exactly as it was,
There in the upper chamber in the ell,
A sort of catchall full of attic clutter.
I often think of the smooth hickory bars.
It got so I would say—you know, half fooling—   145
"It's time I took my turn upstairs in jail"—
Just as you will till it becomes a habit.
No wonder I was glad to get away.
Mind you, I waited till Len said the word.
I didn't want the blame if things went wrong.   150
I was glad though, no end, when we moved out,
And I looked to be happy, and I was,
As I said, for a while—but I don't know!
Somehow the change wore out like a prescription.
And there's more to it than just window views   155
And living by a lake. I'm past such help—
Unless Len took the notion, which he won't,
And I won't ask him—it's not sure enough.
I s'pose I've got to go the road I'm going:
Other folks have to, and why shouldn't I?   160
I almost think if I could do like you,
Drop everything and live out on the ground—
But it might be, come night, I shouldn't like it,
Or a long rain. I should soon get enough,
And be glad of a good roof overhead.   165
I've lain awake thinking of you, I'll warrant,
More than you have yourself, some of these nights.
The wonder was the tents weren't snatched away
From over you as you lay in your beds.
I haven't courage for a risk like that.   170
Bless you, of course you're keeping me from work,

But the thing of it is, I need to *be* kept.
There's work enough to do—there's always that;
But behind's behind. The worst that you can do
Is set me back a little more behind.   175
I shan't catch up in this world, anyway.
I'd *rather* you'd not go unless you must.

AFTER APPLE-PICKING

My long two-pointed ladder's sticking through a tree
Toward heaven still,
And there's a barrel that I didn't fill
Beside it, and there may be two or three
Apples I didn't pick upon some bough.   5
But I am done with apple-picking now.
Essence of winter sleep is on the night,
The scent of apples: I am drowsing off.
I cannot rub the strangeness from my sight
I got from looking through a pane of glass   10
I skimmed this morning from the drinking trough
And held against the world of hoary grass.
It melted, and I let it fall and break.
But I was well
Upon my way to sleep before it fell,   15
And I could tell
What form my dreaming was about to take.
Magnified apples appear and disappear,
Stem end and blossom end,
And every fleck of russet showing clear.   20
My instep arch not only keeps the ache,
It keeps the pressure of a ladder-round.
I feel the ladder sway as the boughs bend.

And I keep hearing from the cellar bin
The rumbling sound   25
Of load on load of apples coming in.
For I have had too much
Of apple-picking: I am overtired
Of the great harvest I myself desired.
There were ten thousand thousand fruit to touch,   30
Cherish in hand, lift down, and not let fall.
For all
That struck the earth,
No matter if not bruised or spiked with stubble,
Went surely to the cider-apple heap   35
As of no worth.
One can see what will trouble
This sleep of mine, whatever sleep it is.
Were he not gone,
The woodchuck could say whether it's like his   40
Long sleep, as I describe its coming on,
Or just some human sleep.

THE CODE

There were three in the meadow by the brook
Gathering up windrows, piling cocks of hay,
With an eye always lifted toward the west
Where an irregular sun-bordered cloud
Darkly advanced with a perpetual dagger   5
Flickering across its bosom. Suddenly
One helper, thrusting pitchfork in the ground,
Marched himself off the field and home. One stayed.
The town-bred farmer failed to understand.

"What is there wrong?"

69

                                  "Something you just now said." 10

"What did I say?"

                    "About our taking pains."

"To cock the hay?—because it's going to shower?
I said that more than half an hour ago.
I said it to myself as much as you."

"You didn't know. But James is one big fool.   15
He thought you meant to find fault with his work.
That's what the average farmer would have meant.
James would take time, of course, to chew it over
Before he acted: he's just got round to act."

"He *is* a fool if that's the way he takes me."   20

"Don't let it bother you. You've found out something.
The hand that knows his business won't be told
To do work better or faster—those two things.
I'm as particular as anyone:
Most likely I'd have served you just the same.   25
But I know you don't understand our ways.
You were just talking what was in your mind,
What was in all our minds, and you weren't hinting.
Tell you a story of what happened once:
I was up here in Salem, at a man's   30
Named Sanders, with a gang of four or five
Doing the haying. No one liked the boss.
He was one of the kind sports call a spider,
All wiry arms and legs that spread out wavy
From a humped body nigh as big's a biscuit.   35
But work! that man could work, especially
If by so doing he could get more work
Out of his hired help. I'm not denying

70

He was hard on himself. I couldn't find
That he kept any hours—not for himself.   40
Daylight and lantern-light were one to him:
I've heard him pounding in the barn all night.
But what he liked was someone to encourage.
Them that he couldn't lead he'd get behind
And drive, the way you can, you know, in mowing—   45
Keep at their heels and threaten to mow their legs off.
I'd seen about enough of his bulling tricks
(We call that bulling). I'd been watching him.
So when he paired off with me in the hayfield
To load the load, thinks I, Look out for trouble.   50
I built the load and topped it off; old Sanders
Combed it down with a rake and says, 'O.K.'
Everything went well till we reached the barn
With a big jag to empty in a bay.
You understand that meant the easy job   55
For the man up on top, of throwing *down*
The hay and rolling it off wholesale,
Where on a mow it would have been slow lifting.
You wouldn't think a fellow'd need much urging
Under those circumstances, would you now?   60
But the old fool seizes his fork in both hands,
And looking up bewhiskered out of the pit,
Shouts like an army captain, 'Let her come!'
Thinks I, D'ye mean it? 'What was that you said?'
I asked out loud, so's there'd be no mistake,   65
'Did you say, "Let her come"?' 'Yes, let her come.'
He said it over, but he said it softer.
Never you say a thing like that to a man,
Not if he values what he is. God, I'd as soon
Murdered him as left out his middle name.   70
I'd built the load and knew right where to find it.

71

Two or three forkfuls I picked lightly round for
Like meditating, and then I just dug in
And dumped the rackful on him in ten lots.
I looked over the side once in the dust   75
And caught sight of him treading-water-like,
Keeping his head above. 'Damn ye,' I says,
'That gets ye!' He squeaked like a squeezed rat.
That was the last I saw or heard of him.
I cleaned the rack and drove out to cool off.   80
As I sat mopping hayseed from my neck,
And sort of waiting to be asked about it,
One of the boys sings out, 'Where's the old man?'
'I left him in the barn under the hay.
If ye want him, ye can go and dig him out.'   85
They realized from the way I swabbed my neck
More than was needed, something must be up.
They headed for the barn; I stayed where I was.
They told me afterward. First they forked hay,
A lot of it, out into the barn floor.   90
Nothing! They listened for him. Not a rustle.
I guess they thought I'd spiked him in the temple
Before I buried him, or I couldn't have managed.
They excavated more. 'Go keep his wife
Out of the barn.' Someone looked in a window,   95
And curse me if he wasn't in the kitchen
Slumped way down in a chair, with both his feet
Against the stove, the hottest day that summer.
He looked so clean disgusted from behind
There was no one that dared to stir him up,   100
Or let him know that he was being looked at.
Apparently I hadn't buried him
(I may have knocked him down); but my just trying
To bury him had hurt his dignity.

72

He had gone to the house so's not to meet me.　　　105
He kept away from us all afternoon.
We tended to his hay. We saw him out
After a while picking peas in his garden:
He couldn't keep away from doing something."

"Weren't you relieved to find he wasn't dead?"　　　110

"No! and yet I don't know—it's hard to say.
I went about to kill him fair enough."

"You took an awkward way. Did he discharge you?"

"Discharge me? No! He knew I did just right."

THE GENERATIONS OF MEN

A governor it was proclaimed this time,
When all who would come seeking in New Hampshire
Ancestral memories might come together.
And those of the name Stark gathered in Bow,
A rock-strewn town where farming has fallen off,　　　5
And sprout-lands flourish where the ax has gone.
Someone had literally run to earth
In an old cellar hole in a byroad
The origin of all the family there.
Thence they were sprung, so numerous a tribe　　　10
That now not all the houses left in town
Made shift to shelter them without the help
Of here and there a tent in grove and orchard.
They were at Bow, but that was not enough:
Nothing would do but they must fix a day　　　15
To stand together on the crater's verge
That turned them on the world, and try to fathom
The past and get some strangeness out of it.

73

But rain spoiled all. The day began uncertain,   19
With clouds low-trailing and moments of rain that misted.
The young folk held some hope out to each other
Till well toward noon, when the storm settled down
With a swish in the grass. "What if the others
Are there," they said. "It isn't going to rain."
Only one from a farm not far away   25
Strolled thither, not expecting he would find
Anyone else, but out of idleness.
One, and one other, yes, for there were two.
The second round the curving hillside road
Was a girl; and she halted some way off   30
To reconnoiter, and then made up her mind
At least to pass by and see who he was,
And perhaps hear some word about the weather.
This was some Stark she didn't know. He nodded.
"No fête today," he said.

                            "It looks that way."   35
She swept the heavens, turning on her heel.
"I only idled down."

                       "I idled down."

Provision there had been for just such meeting
Of stranger-cousins, in a family tree
Drawn on a sort of passport with the branch   40
Of the one bearing it done in detail—
Some zealous one's laborious device.
She made a sudden movement toward her bodice,
As one who clasps her heart. They laughed together.

"Stark?" he inquired. "No matter for the proof."   45

"Yes, Stark. And you?"

74

"I'm Stark." He drew his passport.

"You know we might not be and still be cousins:
The town is full of Chases, Lowes, and Baileys,
All claiming some priority in Starkness.
My mother was a Lane, yet might have married   50
Anyone upon earth and still her children
Would have been Starks, and doubtless here today."

"You riddle with your genealogy,
Like a Viola. I don't follow you."

"I only mean my mother was a Stark   55
Several times over, and by marrying father
No more than brought us back into the name."

"One ought not to be thrown into confusion
By a plain statement of relationship,
But I own what you say makes my head spin.   60
You take my card—you seem so good at such things—
And see if you can reckon our cousinship.
Why not take seats here on the cellar wall
And dangle feet among the raspberry vines?"

"Under the shelter of the family tree."   65

"Just so—that ought to be enough protection."

"Not from the rain. I think it's going to rain."

"It's raining."

         "No, it's misting; let's be fair.
Does the rain seem to you to cool the eyes?"

The situation was like this: the road   70
Bowed outward on the mountain halfway up,
And disappeared and ended not far off.

75

No one went home that way. The only house
Beyond where they were was a shattered seedpod.
And below roared a brook hidden in trees,   75
The sound of which was silence for the place.
This he sat listening to till she gave judgment.

"On father's side, it seems, we're—let me see——"

"Don't be too technical.—You have three cards."

"Four cards: one yours, three mine (one for each branch
Of the Stark family I'm a member of)."   81

"D'you know a person so related to herself
Is supposed to be mad."

                              "I may be mad."

"You look so, sitting out here in the rain
Studying genealogy with me   85
You never saw before. What will we come to
With all this pride of ancestry, we Yankees?
I think we're all mad. Tell me why we're here,
Drawn into town about this cellar hole
Like wild geese on a lake before a storm?   90
What do we see in such a hole, I wonder."

"The Indians had a myth of Chicamoztoc,
Which means The-Seven-Caves-that-We-Came-Out-of.
This is the pit from which we Starks were digged."

"You must be learned. That's what you see in it?"   95

"And what do you see?"

                         "Yes, what *do* I see?
First let me look. I see raspberry vines——"
"Oh, if you're going to use your eyes, just hear

What *I* see. It's a little, little boy,
As pale and dim as a match flame in the sun;   100
He's groping in the cellar after jam—
He thinks it's dark, and it's flooded with daylight."

"He's nothing. Listen. When I lean like this
I can make out old Grandsir Stark distinctly—
With his pipe in his mouth and his brown jug—   105
Bless you, it isn't Grandsir Stark, it's Granny;
But the pipe's there and smoking, and the jug.
She's after cider, the old girl, she's thirsty;
Here's hoping she gets her drink and gets out safely."

"Tell me about her. Does she look like me?"   110

"She should, shouldn't she?—you're so many times
Over descended from her. I believe
She does look like you. Stay the way you are.
The nose is just the same, and so's the chin—
Making allowance, making due allowance."   115

"You poor, dear, great, great, great, great Granny!"

"See that you get her greatness right. Don't stint her."

"Yes, it's important, though you think it isn't.
I won't be teased. But see how wet I am."

"Yes, you must go; we can't stay here forever.   120
But wait until I give you a hand up.
A bead of silver water more or less,
Strung on your hair, won't hurt your summer looks.
I wanted to try something with the noise
That the brook raises in the empty valley.   125
We have seen visions—now consult the voices.
Something I must have learned riding in trains

77

When I was young. I used to use the roar
To set the voices speaking out of it,
Speaking or singing, and the band-music playing. 130
Perhaps you have the art of what I mean.
I've never listened in among the sounds
That a brook makes in such a wild descent.
It ought to give a purer oracle."

"It's as you throw a picture on a screen: 135
The meaning of it all is out of you;
The voices give you what you wish to hear."

"Strangely, it's anything they wish to give."

"Then I don't know. It must be strange enough.
I wonder if it's not your make-believe. 140
What do you think you're like to hear today?"

"From the sense of our having been together—
But why take time for what I'm like to hear?
I'll tell you what the voices really say.
You will do very well right where you are 145
A little longer. I mustn't feel too hurried,
Or I can't give myself to hear the voices."

"Is this some trance you are withdrawing into?"

"You must be very still; you mustn't talk."

"I'll hardly breathe."

     "The voices seem to say——" 150

"I'm waiting."

    "Don't! The voices seem to say:
Call her Nausicaä, the unafraid
Of an acquaintance made adventurously."

78

"I let you say that—on consideration."

"I don't see very well how you can help it.   155
You want the truth. I speak but by the voices.
You see they know I haven't had your name,
Though what a name should matter between us——"

"I shall suspect——"

                    "Be good. The voices say:
Call her Nausicaä, and take a timber   160
That you shall find lies in the cellar, charred
Among the raspberries, and hew and shape it
For a doorsill or other corner piece
In a new cottage on the ancient spot.
The life is not yet all gone out of it.   165
And come and make your summer dwelling here,
And perhaps she will come, still unafraid,
And sit before you in the open door
With flowers in her lap until they fade,
But not come in across the sacred sill——"   170

"I wonder where your oracle is tending.
You can see that there's something wrong with it,
Or it would speak in dialect. Whose voice
Does it purport to speak in? Not old Grandsir's
Nor Granny's, surely. Call up one of them.   175
They have best right to be heard in this place."

"You seem so partial to our great-grandmother
(Nine times removed. Correct me if I err.)
You will be likely to regard as sacred
Anything she may say. But let me warn you,   180
Folks in her day were given to plain speaking.
You think you'd best tempt her at such a time?"

79

"It rests with us always to cut her off."

"Well then, it's Granny speaking: 'I dunnow!
Mebbe I'm wrong to take it as I do.   185
There ain't no names quite like the old ones, though,
Nor never will be to my way of thinking.
One mustn't bear too hard on the newcomers,
But there's a dite too many of them for comfort.
I should feel easier if I could see   190
More of the salt wherewith they're to be salted.
Son, you do as you're told! You take the timber—
It's as sound as the day when it was cut—
And begin over——' There, she'd better stop.
You can see what is troubling Granny, though.   195
But don't you think we sometimes make too much
Of the old stock? What counts is the ideals,
And those will bear some keeping still about."

"I can see we are going to be good friends."

"I like your 'going to be.' You said just now   200
It's going to rain."

                    "I know, and it was raining.
I let you say all that. But I must go now."

"You let me say it? on consideration?
How shall we say good-by in such a case?"

"How shall we?"

                    "Will you leave the way to me?"   205

"No, I don't trust your eyes. You've said enough.
Now give me your hand up.—Pick me that flower."

"Where shall we meet again?"

80

             "Nowhere but here
Once more before we meet elsewhere."

                      "In rain?"

"It ought to be in rain. Sometime in rain.   210
In rain tomorrow, shall we, if it rains?
But if we must, in sunshine." So she went.

THE HOUSEKEEPER

I let myself in at the kitchen door.

"It's you," she said. "I can't get up. Forgive me
Not answering your knock. I can no more
Let people in than I can keep them out.
I'm getting too old for my size, I tell them.   5
My fingers are about all I've the use of
So's to take any comfort. I can sew:
I help out with this beadwork what I can."

"That's a smart pair of pumps you're beading there.
Who are they for?"

                "You mean?—oh, for some miss.   10
I can't keep track of other people's daughters.
Lord, if I were to dream of everyone
Whose shoes I primped to dance in!"

                      "And where's John?"

"Haven't you seen him? Strange what set you off
To come to his house when he's gone to yours.   15
You can't have passed each other. I know what:
He must have changed his mind and gone to Garland's.
He won't be long in that case. You can wait.
Though what good you can be, or anyone—

It's gone so far. You've heard? Estelle's run off." 20

"Yes, what's it all about? When did she go?"

"Two weeks since."

     "She's in earnest, it appears."

"I'm sure she won't come back. She's hiding somewhere.
I don't know where myself. John thinks I do.
He thinks I only have to say the word, 25
And she'll come back. But, bless you, I'm her mother—
I can't talk to her, and, Lord, if I could!"

"It will go hard with John. What will he do?
He can't find anyone to take her place."

"Oh, if you ask me that, what *will* he do? 30
He gets some sort of bakeshop meals together,
With me to sit and tell him everything,
What's wanted and how much and where it is.
But when I'm gone—of course I can't stay here:
Estelle's to take me when she's settled down. 35
He and I only hinder one another.
I tell them they can't get me through the door, though:
I've been built in here like a big church organ.
We've been here fifteen years."

       "That's a long time
To live together and then pull apart. 40
How do you see him living when you're gone?
Two of you out will leave an empty house."

"I don't just see him living many years,
Left here with nothing but the furniture.
I hate to think of the old place when we're gone, 45
With the brook going by below the yard,

82

And no one here but hens blowing about.
If he could sell the place, but then, he can't:
No one will ever live on it again.
It's too run down. This is the last of it.   50
What I think he will do, is let things smash.
He'll sort of swear the time away. He's awful!
I never saw a man let family troubles
Make so much difference in his man's affairs.
He's just dropped everything. He's like a child.   55
I blame his being brought up by his mother.
He's got hay down that's been rained on three times.
He hoed a little yesterday for me:
I thought the growing things would do him good.
Something went wrong. I saw him throw the hoe   60
Sky-high with both hands. I can see it now—
Come here—I'll show you—in that apple tree.
That's no way for a man to do at his age:
He's fifty-five, you know, if he's a day."

"Aren't you afraid of him? What's that gun for?"   65

"Oh, that's been there for hawks since chicken-time.
John Hall touch me! Not if he knows his friends.
I'll say that for him, John's no threatener
Like some menfolk. No one's afraid of him;
All is, he's made up his mind not to stand   70
What he has got to stand."

                        "Where is Estelle?
Couldn't one talk to her? What does she say?
You say you don't know where she is."

                                     "Nor want to!
She thinks if it was bad to live with him,
It must be right to leave him."

"Yes, but he should have married her."

                                        "I know."

"The strain's been too much for her all these years:
I can't explain it any other way.
It's different with a man, at least with John:
He knows he's kinder than the run of men.   80
Better than married ought to be as good
As married—that's what he has always said.
I know the way he's felt—but all the same!"

"I wonder why he doesn't marry her
And end it."

                    "Too late now: she wouldn't have him.   85
He's given her time to think of something else.
That's his mistake. The dear knows my interest
Has been to keep the thing from breaking up.
This is a good home: I don't ask for better.
But when I've said, Why shouldn't they be married?   90
He'd say, Why should they?—no more words than that."

"And after all why should they? John's been fair
I take it. What was his was always hers.
There was no quarrel about property."

"Reason enough, there was no property.   95
A friend or two as good as own the farm,
Such as it is. It isn't worth the mortgage."

"I mean Estelle has always held the purse."

"The rights of that are harder to get at.
I guess Estelle and I have filled the purse.   100
'Twas we let him have money, not he us.

John's a bad farmer. I'm not blaming him.
Take it year in, year out, he doesn't make much.
We came here for a home for me, you know,
Estelle to do the housework for the board   105
Of both of us. But look how it turns out:
She seems to have the housework, and besides,
Half of the outdoor work, though as for that,
He'd say she does it more because she likes it.
You see our pretty things are all outdoors.   110
Our hens and cows and pigs are always better
Than folks like us have any business with.
Farmers around twice as well off as we
Haven't as good. They don't go with the farm.
One thing you can't help liking about John,   115
He's fond of nice things—too fond, some would say.
But Estelle don't complain: she's like him there.
She wants our hens to be the best there are.
You never saw this room before a show,
Full of lank, shivery, half-drowned birds   120
In separate coops, having their plumage done.
The smell of the wet feathers in the heat!
You spoke of John's not being safe to stay with.
You don't know what a gentle lot we are:
We wouldn't hurt a hen! You ought to see us   125
Moving a flock of hens from place to place.
We're not allowed to take them upside down,
All we can hold together by the legs.
Two at a time's the rule, one on each arm,
No matter how far and how many times   130
We have to go."

    "You mean that's John's idea."

"And we live up to it; or I don't know

85

What childishness he wouldn't give way to.
He manages to keep the upper hand
On his own farm. He's boss. But as to hens: 135
We fence our flowers in and the hens range.
Nothing's too good for them. We say it pays.
John likes to tell the offers he has had,
Twenty for this cock, twenty-five for that.
He never takes the money. If they're worth   140
That much to sell, they're worth as much to keep.
Bless you, it's all expense, though. Reach me down
The little tin box on the cupboard shelf—
The upper shelf, the tin box. That's the one.
I'll show you. Here you are."

                "What's this?"

                        "A bill—   145

For fifty dollars for one Langshang cock—
Receipted. And the cock is in the yard."

"Not in a glass case, then?"

                "He'd need a tall one:
He can eat off a barrel from the ground.
He's been in a glass case, as you may say,   150
The Crystal Palace, London. He's imported.
John bought him, and we paid the bill with beads—
Wampum, I call it. Mind, we don't complain.
But you see, don't you, we take care of him."

"And like it, too. It makes it all the worse."   155

"It seems as if. And that's not all: he's helpless
In ways that I can hardly tell you of.
Sometimes he gets possessed to keep accounts
To see where all the money goes so fast.

You know how men will be ridiculous.   160
But it's just fun the way he gets bedeviled—
If he's untidy now, what will he be——?"

"It makes it all the worse. You must be blind."

"Estelle's the one. You needn't talk to me."

"Can't you and I get to the root of it?   165
What's the real trouble? What will satisfy her?"

"It's as I say: she's turned from him, that's all."

"But why, when she's well off? Is it the neighbors,
Being cut off from friends?"

                            "We have our friends.
That isn't it. Folks aren't afraid of us."   170

"She's let it worry her. You stood the strain,
And you're her mother."

                        "But I didn't always.
I didn't relish it along at first.
But I got wonted to it. And besides—
John said I was too old to have grandchildren.   175
But what's the use of talking when it's done?
She won't come back—it's worse than that—she can't."

"Why do you speak like that? What do you know?
What do you mean?—she's done harm to herself?"

"I mean she's married—married someone else."   180

"Oho, oho!"

             "You don't believe me."

                          "Yes, I do,
Only too well. I knew there must be something!

87

So that was what was back. She's bad, that's all!"

"Bad to get married when she had the chance?"   184

"Nonsense! See what she's done! But who, but who——?"

"Who'd marry her straight out of such a mess?
Say it right out—no matter for her mother.
The man was found. I'd better name no names.
John himself won't imagine who he is."

"Then it's all up. I think I'll get away.   190
You'll be expecting John. I pity Estelle;
I suppose she deserves some pity, too.
You ought to have the kitchen to yourself
To break it to him. You may have the job."

"You needn't think you're going to get away.   195
John's almost here. I've had my eye on someone
Coming down Ryan's Hill. I thought 'twas him.
Here he is now. This box! Put it away.
And this bill."

        "What's the hurry? He'll unhitch."

"No, he won't, either. He'll just drop the reins   200
And turn Doll out to pasture, rig and all.
She won't get far before the wheels hang up
On something—there's no harm. See, there he is!
My, but he looks as if he must have heard!"

John threw the door wide but he didn't enter.   205
"How are you, neighbor? Just the man I'm after.
Isn't it Hell?" he said. "I want to know.
Come out here if you want to hear me talk.—
I'll talk to you, old woman, afterward.—
I've got some news that maybe isn't news.   210

What are they trying to do to me, these two?"

"Do go along with him and stop his shouting."
She raised her voice against the closing door:
"Who wants to hear your news, you—dreadful fool?"

THE FEAR

A lantern-light from deeper in the barn
Shone on a man and woman in the door
And threw their lurching shadows on a house
Nearby, all dark in every glossy window.
A horse's hoof pawed once the hollow floor,   5
And the back of the gig they stood beside
Moved in a little. The man grasped a wheel.
The woman spoke out sharply, "Whoa, stand still!—
I saw it just as plain as a white plate,"
She said, "as the light on the dashboard ran   10
Along the bushes at the roadside—a man's face.
You *must* have seen it too."
                              "I didn't see it.
Are you sure——"
                      "Yes, I'm sure!"
                                      "—it was a face?"

"Joel, I'll have to look. I can't go in,
I can't, and leave a thing like that unsettled.   15
Doors locked and curtains drawn will make no difference.
I always have felt strange when we came home
To the dark house after so long an absence,
And the key rattled loudly into place
Seemed to warn someone to be getting out   20
At one door as we entered at another.

What if I'm right, and someone all the time—
Don't hold my arm!"

        "I say it's someone passing."

"You speak as if this were a traveled road.
You forget where we are. What is beyond   25
That he'd be going to or coming from
At such an hour of night, and on foot too?
What was he standing still for in the bushes?"

"It's not so very late—it's only dark.
There's more in it than you're inclined to say.   30
Did he look like——?"

        "He looked like anyone.
I'll never rest tonight unless I know.
Give me the lantern."

        "You don't want the lantern."

She pushed past him and got it for herself.

"You're not to come," she said. "This is my business. 35
If the time's come to face it, I'm the one
To put it the right way. He'd never dare—
Listen! He kicked a stone. Hear that, hear that!
He's coming towards us. Joel, *go* in—please.
Hark!—I don't hear him now. But please go in."   40

"In the first place you can't make me believe it's——"

"It is—or someone else he's sent to watch.
And now's the time to have it out with him
While we know definitely where he is.
Let him get off and he'll be everywhere   45
Around us, looking out of trees and bushes
Till I shan't dare to set a foot outdoors.

90

And I can't stand it. Joel, let me go!"

"But it's nonsense to think he'd care enough."

"You mean you couldn't understand his caring.   50
Oh, but you see he hadn't had enough—
Joel, I won't—I won't—I promise you.
We mustn't say hard things. You mustn't either."

"I'll be the one, if anybody goes!
But you give him the advantage with this light.   55
What couldn't he do to us standing here!
And if to see was what he wanted, why,
He has seen all there was to see and gone."

He appeared to forget to keep his hold,
But advanced with her as she crossed the grass.   60

"What do you want?" she cried to all the dark.
She stretched up tall to overlook the light
That hung in both hands, hot against her skirt.

"There's no one; so you're wrong," he said.
                                "There is.—
What do you want?" she cried, and then herself   65
Was startled when an answer really came.

"Nothing." It came from well along the road.

She reached a hand to Joel for support:
The smell of scorching woolen made her faint.
"What are you doing round this house at night?"   70

"Nothing." A pause: there seemed no more to say.

And then the voice again: "You seem afraid.
I saw by the way you whipped up the horse.
I'll just come forward in the lantern-light

91

And let you see."

          "Yes, do.—Joel, go back!"   75

She stood her ground against the noisy steps
That came on, but her body rocked a little.

"You see," the voice said.

          "Oh." She looked and looked.

"You don't see—I've a child here by the hand.
A robber wouldn't have his family with him."   80

"What's a child doing at this time of night——?"

"Out walking. Every child should have the memory
Of at least one long-after-bedtime walk.
What, son?"

       "Then I should think you'd try to find   84
Somewhere to walk——"

        "The highway, as it happens—
We're stopping for the fortnight down at Dean's."

"But if that's all—Joel—you realize—
You won't think anything. You understand?
You understand that we have to be careful.
This is a very, very lonely place.—   90
Joel!" She spoke as if she couldn't turn.
The swinging lantern lengthened to the ground,
It touched, it struck, it clattered and went out.

THE SELF-SEEKER

"Willis, I didn't want you here today:
The lawyer's coming for the company.
I'm going to sell my soul, or rather, feet.

92

Five hundred dollars for the pair, you know."

"With you the feet have nearly been the soul;   5
And if you're going to sell them to the devil,
I want to see you do it. When's he coming?"

"I half suspect you knew, and came on purpose
To try to help me drive a better bargain."

"Well, if it's true! Yours are no common feet.   10
The lawyer don't know what it is he's buying:
So many miles you might have walked you won't walk.
You haven't run your forty orchids down.
What does he think?—How *are* the blessèd feet?
The doctor's sure you're going to walk again?"   15

"He thinks I'll hobble. It's both legs and feet."

"They must be terrible—I mean, to look at."

"I haven't dared to look at them uncovered.
Through the bed blankets I remind myself
Of a starfish laid out with rigid points."   20

"The wonder is it hadn't been your head."

"It's hard to tell you how I managed it.
When I saw the shaft had me by the coat,
I didn't try too long to pull away,
Or fumble for my knife to cut away,   25
I just embraced the shaft and rode it out—
Till Weiss shut off the water in the wheel pit.
That's how I think I didn't lose my head.
But my legs got their knocks against the ceiling."

"Awful. Why didn't they throw off the belt   30
Instead of going clear down in the wheel pit?"

93

"They say some time was wasted on the belt—
Old streak of leather—doesn't love me much
Because I make him spit fire at my knuckles,
The way Ben Franklin used to make the kite string.   35
That must be it. Some days he won't stay on.
That day a woman couldn't coax him off.
He's on his rounds now with his tail in his mouth,
Snatched right and left across the silver pulleys.
Everything goes the same without me there.   40
You can hear the small buzz saws whine, the big saw
Caterwaul to the hills around the village
As they both bite the wood. It's all our music.
One ought as a good villager to like it.
No doubt it has a sort of prosperous sound,   45
And it's our life."

                 "Yes, when it's not our death."

"You make that sound as if it wasn't so
With everything. What we live by we die by.—
I wonder where my lawyer is. His train's in.
I want this over with; I'm hot and tired."   50

"You're getting ready to do something foolish."

"Watch for him, will you, Will? You let him in.
I'd rather Mrs. Corbin didn't know;
I've boarded here so long, she thinks she owns me.
You're bad enough to manage, without her."   55

"I'm going to be worse instead of better.
You've got to tell me how far this is gone:
Have you agreed to any price?"

                     "Five hundred.
Five hundred—five—five! One, two, three, four, five.

94

You needn't look at me."

                "I don't believe you."   60

"I told you, Willis, when you first came in.
Don't you be hard on me. I have to take
What I can get. You see they have the feet,
Which gives them the advantage in the trade.
I can't get back the feet in any case."   65

"But your flowers, man, you're selling out your flowers."

"Yes, that's one way to put it—all the flowers
Of every kind everywhere in this region
For the next forty summers—call it forty.
But I'm not selling those, I'm giving them;   70
They never earned me so much as one cent:
Money can't pay me for the loss of them.
No, the five hundred was the sum they named
To pay the doctor's bill and tide me over.
It's that or fight, and I don't want to fight—   75
I just want to get settled in my life,
Such as it's going to be, and know the worst,
Or best—it may not be so bad. The firm
Promise me all the shooks I want to nail."

"But what about your flora of the valley?"   80

"You have me there. But that—you didn't think
That was worth money to me? Still I own
It goes against me not to finish it
For the friends it might bring me. By the way,
I had a letter from Burroughs—did I tell you?—   85
About my *Cypripedium reginæ*;
He says it's not reported so far north.—
There! there's the bell. He's rung. But you go down

And bring him up, and don't let Mrs. Corbin.—
Oh, well, we'll soon be through with it. I'm tired."   90

Willis brought up besides the Boston lawyer
A little barefoot girl, who in the noise
Of heavy footsteps in the old frame house,
And baritone importance of the lawyer,
Stood for a while unnoticed, with her hands   95
Shyly behind her.

        "Well, and how is Mister . . . ?"
The lawyer was already in his satchel
As if for papers that might bear the name
He hadn't at command. "You must excuse me,
I dropped in at the mill and was detained."   100

"Looking round, I suppose," said Willis.

                  "Yes,
Well, yes."

       "Hear anything that might prove useful?"

The Broken One saw Anne. "Why, here is Anne.
What do you want, dear? Come, stand by the bed;
Tell me what is it?"

        Anne just wagged her dress,   105
With both hands held behind her. "Guess," she said.

"Oh, guess which hand? My, my! Once on a time
I knew a lovely way to tell for certain
By looking in the ears. But I forget it.
Er, let me see. I think I'll take the right.   110
That's sure to be right, even if it's wrong.
Come, hold it out. Don't change.—A Ram's Horn orchid!
A Ram's Horn! What would I have got, I wonder,

If I had chosen left. Hold out the left.
Another Ram's Horn! Where did you find those,   115
Under what beech tree, on what woodchuck's knoll?"

Anne looked at the large lawyer at her side,
And thought she wouldn't venture on so much.

"Were there no others?"

                              "There were four or five.
I knew you wouldn't let me pick them all."   120

"I wouldn't—so I wouldn't. You're the girl!
You see Anne has her lesson learned by heart."

"I wanted there should be some there next year."

"Of course you did. You left the rest for seed,
And for the backwoods woodchuck. You're the girl!   125
A Ram's Horn orchid seedpod for a woodchuck
Sounds something like. Better than farmer's beans
To a discriminating appetite,
Though the Ram's Horn is seldom to be had
In bushel lots—doesn't come on the market.   130
But, Anne, I'm troubled; have you told me all?
You're hiding something. That's as bad as lying.
You ask this lawyer man. And it's not safe
With a lawyer at hand to find you out.
Nothing is hidden from some people, Anne.   135
You don't tell me that where you found a Ram's Horn
You didn't find a Yellow Lady's Slipper.
What did I tell you? What? I'd blush, I would.
Don't you defend yourself. If it was there,
Where is it now, the Yellow Lady's Slipper?"   140

"Well, wait—it's common—it's too *common*."

                              "Common?

97

The Purple Lady's Slipper's commoner."

"I didn't bring a Purple Lady's Slipper.
To *You*—to you I mean—they're both too common."

The lawyer gave a laugh among his papers   145
As if with some idea that she had scored.

"I've broken Anne of gathering bouquets.
It's not fair to the child. It can't be helped, though:
Pressed into service means pressed out of shape.
Somehow I'll make it right with her—she'll see.   150
She's going to do my scouting in the field,
Over stone walls and all along a wood
And by a river bank for water flowers,
The Floating Heart, with small leaf like a heart,
And at the sinus under water a fist   155
Of little fingers all kept down but one,
And that thrust up to blossom in the sun
As if to say, 'You! You're the Heart's desire.'
Anne has a way with flowers to take the place
Of what she's lost: she goes down on one knee   160
And lifts their faces by the chin to hers
And says their names, and leaves them where they are."

The lawyer wore a watch the case of which
Was cunningly devised to make a noise
Like a small pistol when he snapped it shut   165
At such a time as this. He snapped it now.

"Well, Anne, go, dearie. Our affair will wait.
The lawyer man is thinking of his train.
He wants to give me lots and lots of money
Before he goes, because I hurt myself,   170
And it may take him I don't know how long.

98

But put our flowers in water first.—Will, help her:
The pitcher's too full for her.—There's no cup?
Just hook them on the inside of the pitcher.
Now run.—Get out your documents! You see   175
I have to keep on the good side of Anne.
I'm a great boy to think of number one.
And you can't blame me in the place I'm in.
Who will take care of my necessities
Unless I do?"

            "A pretty interlude,"   180
The lawyer said. "I'm sorry, but my train—
Luckily terms are all agreed upon.
You only have to sign your name. Right—there."

"You, Will, stop making faces. Come round here
Where you can't make them. What is it you want?   185
I'll put you out with Anne. Be good or go."

"You don't mean you will sign that thing unread?"

"Make yourself useful, then, and read it for me.—
Isn't it something I have seen before?"

"You'll find it is. Let your friend look at it."   190

"Yes, but all that takes time, and I'm as much
In haste to get it over with as you.—
But read it, read it.—That's right, draw the curtain:
Half the time I don't know what's troubling me.—
What do you say, Will? Don't you be a fool,   195
You, crumpling folks's legal documents.
Out with it if you've any real objection."

"Five hundred dollars!"

            "What would you think right?"

"A thousand wouldn't be a cent too much;
You know it, Mr. Lawyer. The sin is   200
Accepting anything before he knows
Whether he's ever going to walk again.
It smells to me like a dishonest trick."

"I think—I think—from what I heard today—
And saw myself—he would be ill-advised——"   205

"What did you hear, for instance?" Willis said.

"Now, the place where the accident occurred——"

The Broken One was twisted in his bed.
"This is between you two apparently.
Where I come in is what I want to know.   210
You stand up to it like a pair of cocks.
Go outdoors if you want to fight. Spare me.
When you come back, I'll have the papers signed.
Will pencil do? Then, please, your fountain pen.
One of you hold my head up from the pillow."   215

Willis flung off the bed. "I wash my hands—
I'm no match—no, and don't pretend to be——"

The lawyer gravely capped his fountain pen.
"You're doing the wise thing: you won't regret it.
We're very sorry for you."
                             Willis sneered: 220
"Who's *we?*—some stockholders in Boston?
I'll go outdoors, by gad, and won't come back."

"Willis, bring Anne back with you when you come.
Yes. Thanks for caring.—Don't mind Will: he's savage.
He thinks you ought to pay me for my flowers.   225
You don't know what I mean about the flowers.

Don't stop to try to now. You'll miss your train.
Good-by." He flung his arms around his face.

THE WOOD-PILE

Out walking in the frozen swamp one gray day,
I paused and said, "I will turn back from here.
No, I will go on farther—and we shall see."
The hard snow held me, save where now and then
One foot went through. The view was all in lines   5
Straight up and down of tall slim trees
Too much alike to mark or name a place by
So as to say for certain I was here
Or somewhere else: I was just far from home.
A small bird flew before me. He was careful   10
To put a tree between us when he lighted,
And say no word to tell me who he was
Who was so foolish as to think what *he* thought.
He thought that I was after him for a feather—
The white one in his tail; like one who takes   15
Everything said as personal to himself.
One flight out sideways would have undeceived him.
And then there was a pile of wood for which
I forgot him and let his little fear
Carry him off the way I might have gone,   20
Without so much as wishing him good-night.
He went behind it to make his last stand.
It was a cord of maple, cut and split
And piled—and measured, four by four by eight.
And not another like it could I see.   25
No runner tracks in this year's snow looped near it.
And it was older sure than this year's cutting,
Or even last year's or the year's before.

101

The wood was gray and the bark warping off it
And the pile somewhat sunken. Clematis   30
Had wound strings round and round it like a bundle.
What held it, though, on one side was a tree
Still growing, and on one a stake and prop,
These latter about to fall. I thought that only
Someone who lived in turning to fresh tasks   35
Could so forget his handiwork on which
He spent himself, the labor of his ax,
And leave it there far from a useful fireplace
To warm the frozen swamp as best it could
With the slow smokeless burning of decay.   40

GOOD HOURS

I had for my winter evening walk—
No one at all with whom to talk,
But I had the cottages in a row
Up to their shining eyes in snow.

And I thought I had the folk within: 5
I had the sound of a violin;
I had a glimpse through curtain laces
Of youthful forms and youthful faces.

I had such company outward bound.
I went till there were no cottages found.   10
I turned and repented, but coming back
I saw no window but that was black.

Over the snow my creaking feet
Disturbed the slumbering village street
Like profanation, by your leave,   15
At ten o'clock of a winter eve.

102

Mountain Interval

: 1916 :

THE ROAD NOT TAKEN

Two roads diverged in a yellow wood,
And sorry I could not travel both
And be one traveler, long I stood
And looked down one as far as I could
To where it bent in the undergrowth;   5

Then took the other, as just as fair,
And having perhaps the better claim,
Because it was grassy and wanted wear;
Though as for that, the passing there
Had worn them really about the same,   10

And both that morning equally lay
In leaves no step had trodden black.
Oh, I kept the first for another day!
Yet knowing how way leads on to way,
I doubted if I should ever come back.   15

I shall be telling this with a sigh
Somewhere ages and ages hence:
Two roads diverged in a wood, and I—
I took the one less traveled by,
And that has made all the difference.   20

CHRISTMAS TREES

A Christmas circular letter

The city had withdrawn into itself
And left at last the country to the country;

105

When between whirls of snow not come to lie
And whirls of foliage not yet laid, there drove
A stranger to our yard, who looked the city,   5
Yet did in country fashion in that there
He sat and waited till he drew us out,
A-buttoning coats, to ask him who he was.
He proved to be the city come again
To look for something it had left behind   10
And could not do without and keep its Christmas.
He asked if I would sell my Christmas trees;
My woods—the young fir balsams like a place
Where houses all are churches and have spires.
I hadn't thought of them as Christmas trees.   15
I doubt if I was tempted for a moment
To sell them off their feet to go in cars
And leave the slope behind the house all bare,
Where the sun shines now no warmer than the moon.
I'd hate to have them know it if I was.   20
Yet more I'd hate to hold my trees, except
As others hold theirs or refuse for them,
Beyond the time of profitable growth—
The trial by market everything must come to.
I dallied so much with the thought of selling.   25
Then whether from mistaken courtesy
And fear of seeming short of speech, or whether
From hope of hearing good of what was mine,
I said, "There aren't enough to be worth while."

"I could soon tell how many they would cut,   30
You let me look them over."

                              "You could look.
But don't expect I'm going to let you have them."

Pasture they spring in, some in clumps too close
That lop each other of boughs, but not a few
Quite solitary and having equal boughs   35
All round and round. The latter he nodded "Yes" to,
Or paused to say beneath some lovelier one,
With a buyer's moderation, "That would do."
I thought so too, but wasn't there to say so.
We climbed the pasture on the south, crossed over,   40
And came down on the north.

                      He said, "A thousand."

"A thousand Christmas trees!—at what apiece?"

He felt some need of softening that to me:
"A thousand trees would come to thirty dollars."

Then I was certain I had never meant   45
To let him have them. Never show surprise!
But thirty dollars seemed so small beside
The extent of pasture I should strip, three cents
(For that was all they figured out apiece)—
Three cents so small beside the dollar friends   50
I should be writing to within the hour
Would pay in cities for good trees like those,
Regular vestry-trees whole Sunday Schools
Could hang enough on to pick off enough.

A thousand Christmas trees I didn't know I had!   55
Worth three cents more to give away than sell,
As may be shown by a simple calculation.
Too bad I couldn't lay one in a letter.
I can't help wishing I could send you one
In wishing you herewith a Merry Christmas.   60

AN OLD MAN'S WINTER NIGHT

All out-of-doors looked darkly in at him
Through the thin frost, almost in separate stars,
That gathers on the pane in empty rooms.
What kept his eyes from giving back the gaze
Was the lamp tilted near them in his hand.   5
What kept him from remembering what it was
That brought him to that creaking room was age.
He stood with barrels round him—at a loss.
And having scared the cellar under him
In clomping here, he scared it once again   10
In clomping off—and scared the outer night,
Which has its sounds, familiar, like the roar
Of trees and crack of branches, common things,
But nothing so like beating on a box.
A light he was to no one but himself   15
Where now he sat, concerned with he knew what,
A quiet light, and then not even that.
He consigned to the moon—such as she was,
So late-arising—to the broken moon,
As better than the sun in any case   20
For such a charge, his snow upon the roof,
His icicles along the wall to keep;
And slept. The log that shifted with a jolt
Once in the stove, disturbed him and he shifted,
And eased his heavy breathing, but still slept.   25
One aged man—one man—can't keep a house,
A farm, a countryside, or if he can,
It's thus he does it of a winter night.

THE EXPOSED NEST

You were forever finding some new play.
So when I saw you down on hands and knees
In the meadow, busy with the new-cut hay,
Trying, I thought, to set it up on end,
I went to show you how to make it stay,   5
If that was your idea, against the breeze,
And, if you asked me, even help pretend
To make it root again and grow afresh.
But 'twas no make-believe with you today,
Nor was the grass itself your real concern,   10
Though I found your hand full of wilted fern,
Steel-bright June-grass, and blackening heads of clover.
'Twas a nest full of young birds on the ground
The cutter bar had just gone champing over
(Miraculously without tasting flesh)   15
And left defenseless to the heat and light.
You wanted to restore them to their right
Of something interposed between their sight
And too much world at once—could means be found.
The way the nest-full every time we stirred   20
Stood up to us as to a mother-bird
Whose coming home has been too long deferred,
Made me ask would the mother-bird return
And care for them in such a change of scene,
And might our meddling make her more afraid.   25
That was a thing we could not wait to learn.
We saw the risk we took in doing good,
But dared not spare to do the best we could
Though harm should come of it; so built the screen
You had begun, and gave them back their shade.   30
All this to prove we cared. Why is there then

No more to tell? We turned to other things.
I haven't any memory—have you?—
Of ever coming to the place again
To see if the birds lived the first night through,   35
And so at last to learn to use their wings.

A PATCH OF OLD SNOW

There's a patch of old snow in a corner,
  That I should have guessed
Was a blow-away paper the rain
  Had brought to rest.

It is speckled with grime as if   5
  Small print overspread it,
The news of a day I've forgotten—
  If I ever read it.

IN THE HOME STRETCH

She stood against the kitchen sink, and looked
Over the sink out through a dusty window
At weeds the water from the sink made tall.
She wore her cape; her hat was in her hand.
Behind her was confusion in the room,   5
Of chairs turned upside down to sit like people
In other chairs, and something, come to look,
For every room a house has—parlor, bedroom,
And dining room—thrown pell-mell in the kitchen.
And now and then a smudged, infernal face   10
Looked in a door behind her and addressed
Her back. She always answered without turning.

"Where will I put this walnut bureau, lady?"

110

"Put it on top of something that's on top
Of something else," she laughed. "Oh, put it where   15
You can tonight, and go. It's almost dark;
You must be getting started back to town."

Another blackened face thrust in and looked
And smiled, and when she did not turn, spoke gently,
"What are you seeing out the window, *lady*?"   20

"Never was I beladied so before.
Would evidence of having been called lady
More than so many times make me a lady
In common law, I wonder."

                              "But I ask,
What are you seeing out the window, lady?"   25

"What I'll be seeing more of in the years
To come as here I stand and go the round
Of many plates with towels many times."

"And what is that? You only put me off."

"Rank weeds that love the water from the dishpan   30
More than some women like the dishpan, Joe;
A little stretch of mowing field for you;
Not much of that until I come to woods
That end all. And it's scarce enough to call
A view."

                  "And yet you think you like it, dear?"   35

"That's what you're so concerned to know! You hope
I like it.—Bang goes something big away
Off there upstairs. The very tread of men
As great as those is shattering to the frame
Of such a little house. Once left alone,   40
You and I, dear, will go with softer steps

111

Up and down stairs and through the rooms, and none
But sudden winds that snatch them from our hands
Will ever slam the doors."

                 "I think you see
More than you like to own to out that window."   45

"No; for besides the things I tell you of,
I only see the years. They come and go
In alternation with the weeds, the field,
The wood."

          "What kind of years?"

                 "Why, latter years—
Different from early years."

               "I see them, too.   50
You didn't count them?"

               "No, the further off
So ran together that I didn't try to.
It can scarce be that they would be in number
We'd care to know, for we are not young now.—
And bang goes something else away off there.   55
It sounds as if it were the men went down,
And every crash meant one less to return
To lighted city streets we, too, have known,
But now are giving up for country darkness."

"Come from that window where you see too much,   60
And take a livelier view of things from here.
They're going. Watch this husky swarming up
Over the wheel into the sky-high seat,
Lighting his pipe now, squinting down his nose
At the flame burning downward as he sucks it."   65

"See how it makes his nose-side bright, a proof

How dark it's getting. Can you tell what time
It is by that? Or by the moon? The new moon!
What shoulder did I see her over? Neither.
A wire she is of silver, as new as we   70
To everything. Her light won't last us long.
It's something, though, to know we're going to have her
Night after night and stronger every night
To see us through our first two weeks. But, Joe,
The stove! Before they go! Knock on the window;   75
Ask them to help you get it on its feet.
We stand here dreaming. Hurry! Call them back!"

"They're not gone yet."

                      "We've got to have the stove,
Whatever else we want for. And a light.
Have we a piece of candle if the lamp   80
And oil are buried out of reach?"

                         Again
The house was full of tramping, and the dark,
Door-filling men burst in and seized the stove.
A cannon-mouth-like hole was in the wall,
To which they set it true by eye; and then   85
Came up the jointed stovepipe in their hands,
So much too light and airy for their strength
It almost seemed to come ballooning up,
Slipping from clumsy clutches toward the ceiling.
"A fit!" said one, and banged a stovepipe shoulder. 90
"It's good luck when you move in to begin
With good luck with your stovepipe. Never mind,
It's not so bad in the country, settled down,
When people're getting on in life. You'll like it."

Joe said: "You big boys ought to find a farm,   95

113

And make good farmers, and leave other fellows
The city work to do. There's not enough
For everybody as it is in there."

"God!" one said wildly, and, when no one spoke:
"Say that to Jimmy here. He needs a farm."   100
But Jimmy only made his jaw recede
Fool-like, and rolled his eyes as if to say
He saw himself a farmer. Then there was a French boy
Who said with seriousness that made them laugh,
"Ma friend, you ain't know what it is you're ask."   105
He doffed his cap and held it with both hands
Across his chest to make as 'twere a bow:
"We're giving you our chances on de farm."
And then they all turned to with deafening boots
And put each other bodily out of the house.   110

"Good-by to them! We puzzle them. They think—
I don't know what they think we see in what
They leave us to: that pasture slope that seems
The back some farm presents us; and your woods
To northward from your window at the sink,   115
Waiting to steal a step on us whenever
We drop our eyes or turn to other things,
As in the game 'ten-step' the children play."

"Good boys they seemed, and let them love the city.
All they could say was 'God!' when you proposed   120
Their coming out and making useful farmers."

"Did they make something lonesome go through you?
It would take more than them to sicken you—
Us of our bargain. But they left us so
As to our fate, like fools past reasoning with.   125
They almost shook *me*."

114

                "It's all so much
What we have always wanted, I confess
Its seeming bad for a moment makes it seem
Even worse still, and so on down, down, down.
It's nothing; it's their leaving us at dusk.   130
I never bore it well when people went.
The first night after guests have gone, the house
Seems haunted or exposed. I always take
A personal interest in the locking up
At bedtime; but the strangeness soon wears off."   135
He fetched a dingy lantern from behind
A door. "There's that we didn't lose! And these!"—
Some matches he unpocketed. "For food—
The meals we've had no one can take from us.
I wish that everything on earth were just   140
As certain as the meals we've had. I wish
The meals we haven't had were, anyway.
What have you you know where to lay your hands on?"

"The bread we bought in passing at the store.
There's butter somewhere, too."

                        "Let's rend the bread.   145
I'll light the fire for company for you;
You'll not have any other company
Till Ed begins to get out on a Sunday
To look us over and give us his idea
Of what wants pruning, shingling, breaking up.   150
He'll know what he would do if he were we,
And all at once. He'll plan for us and plan
To help us, but he'll take it out in planning.
Well, you can set the table with the loaf.
Let's see you find your loaf. I'll light the fire.   155
I like chairs occupying other chairs

Not offering a lady——"

                    "There again, Joe!
You're tired."

              "I'm drunk-nonsensical tired out;
Don't mind a word I say. It's a day's work
To empty one house of all household goods   160
And fill another with 'em fifteen miles away,
Although you do no more than dump them down."

"Dumped down in paradise we are and happy."

"It's all so much what I have always wanted,
I can't believe it's what you wanted, too."   165

"Shouldn't you like to know?"

                    "I'd like to know
If it is what you wanted, then how much
You wanted it for me."

               "A troubled conscience!
You don't want me to tell if *I* don't know."

"I don't want to find out what can't be known.   170
But who first said the word to come?"

                    "My dear,
It's who first thought the thought. You're searching, Joe,
For things that don't exist; I mean beginnings.
Ends and beginnings—there are no such things.
There are only middles."

               "What is this?"

                    "This life?   175
Our sitting here by lantern-light together
Amid the wreckage of a former home?
You won't deny the lantern isn't new.

116

The stove is not, and you are not to me,
Nor I to you."

        "Perhaps you never were?"   180

"It would take me forever to recite
All that's not new in where we find ourselves.
New is a word for fools in towns who think
Style upon style in dress and thought at last
Must get somewhere. I've heard you say as much.   185
No, this is no beginning."

        "Then an end?"

"End is a gloomy word."

        "Is it too late
To drag you out for just a good-night call
On the old peach trees on the knoll, to grope
By starlight in the grass for a last peach   190
The neighbors may not have taken as their right
When the house wasn't lived in? I've been looking:
I doubt if they have left us many grapes.
Before we set ourselves to right the house,
The first thing in the morning, out we go   195
To go the round of apple, cherry, peach,
Pine, alder, pasture, mowing, well, and brook.
All of a farm it is."

        "I know this much:
I'm going to put you in your bed, if first
I have to make you build it. Come, the light."   200

When there was no more lantern in the kitchen,
The fire got out through crannies in the stove
And danced in yellow wrigglers on the ceiling,
As much at home as if they'd always danced there.

THE TELEPHONE

"When I was just as far as I could walk
From here today,
There was an hour
All still
When leaning with my head against a flower   5
I heard you talk.
Don't say I didn't, for I heard you say—
You spoke from that flower on the windowsill—
Do you remember what it was you said?"

"First tell me what it was you thought you heard."   10

"Having found the flower and driven a bee away,
I leaned my head,
And holding by the stalk,
I listened and I thought I caught the word—
What was it? Did you call me by my name?   15
Or did you say—
Someone said 'Come'—I heard it as I bowed."

"I may have thought as much, but not aloud."

"Well, so I came."

MEETING AND PASSING

As I went down the hill along the wall
There was a gate I had leaned at for the view
And had just turned from when I first saw you
As you came up the hill. We met. But all
We did that day was mingle great and small   5
Footprints in summer dust as if we drew
The figure of our being less than two

118

But more than one as yet. Your parasol
Pointed the decimal off with one deep thrust.
And all the time we talked you seemed to see   10
Something down there to smile at in the dust.
(Oh, it was without prejudice to me!)
Afterward I went past what you had passed
Before we met, and you what I had passed.

HYLA BROOK

By June our brook's run out of song and speed.
Sought for much after that, it will be found
Either to have gone groping underground
(And taken with it all the Hyla breed
That shouted in the mist a month ago,   5
Like ghost of sleigh bells in a ghost of snow)—
Or flourished and come up in jewelweed,
Weak foliage that is blown upon and bent,
Even against the way its waters went.
Its bed is left a faded paper sheet   10
Of dead leaves stuck together by the heat—
A brook to none but who remember long.
This as it will be seen is other far
Than with brooks taken otherwhere in song.
We love the things we love for what they are.   15

THE OVEN BIRD

There is a singer everyone has heard,
Loud, a mid-summer and a mid-wood bird,
Who makes the solid tree trunks sound again.
He says that leaves are old and that for flowers

119

Mid-summer is to spring as one to ten.   5
He says the early petal-fall is past,
When pear and cherry bloom went down in showers
On sunny days a moment overcast;
And comes that other fall we name the fall.
He says the highway dust is over all.   10
The bird would cease and be as other birds
But that he knows in singing not to sing.
The question that he frames in all but words
Is what to make of a diminished thing.

BOND AND FREE

Love has earth to which she clings
With hills and circling arms about—
Wall within wall to shut fear out.
But Thought has need of no such things,
For Thought has a pair of dauntless wings.   5

On snow and sand and turf, I see
Where Love has left a printed trace
With straining in the world's embrace.
And such is Love and glad to be.
But Thought has shaken his ankles free.   10

Thought cleaves the interstellar gloom
And sits in Sirius' disc all night,
Till day makes him retrace his flight,
With smell of burning on every plume,
Back past the sun to an earthly room.   15

His gains in heaven are what they are.
Yet some say Love by being thrall
And simply staying possesses all

120

In several beauty that Thought fares far
To find fused in another star.   20

BIRCHES

When I see birches bend to left and right
Across the lines of straighter darker trees,
I like to think some boy's been swinging them.
But swinging doesn't bend them down to stay
As ice storms do. Often you must have seen them   5
Loaded with ice a sunny winter morning
After a rain. They click upon themselves
As the breeze rises, and turn many-colored
As the stir cracks and crazes their enamel.
Soon the sun's warmth makes them shed crystal shells   10
Shattering and avalanching on the snow crust—
Such heaps of broken glass to sweep away
You'd think the inner dome of heaven had fallen.
They are dragged to the withered bracken by the load,
And they seem not to break; though once they are bowed
So low for long, they never right themselves:
You may see their trunks arching in the woods
Years afterwards, trailing their leaves on the ground
Like girls on hands and knees that throw their hair
Before them over their heads to dry in the sun.   20
But I was going to say when Truth broke in
With all her matter of fact about the ice storm,
I should prefer to have some boy bend them
As he went out and in to fetch the cows—
Some boy too far from town to learn baseball,   25
Whose only play was what he found himself,
Summer or winter, and could play alone.

121

One by one he subdued his father's trees
By riding them down over and over again
Until he took the stiffness out of them,   30
And not one but hung limp, not one was left
For him to conquer. He learned all there was
To learn about not launching out too soon
And so not carrying the tree away
Clear to the ground. He always kept his poise   35
To the top branches, climbing carefully
With the same pains you use to fill a cup
Up to the brim, and even above the brim.
Then he flung outward, feet first, with a swish,
Kicking his way down through the air to the ground.   40
So was I once myself a swinger of birches.
And so I dream of going back to be.
It's when I'm weary of considerations,
And life is too much like a pathless wood
Where your face burns and tickles with the cobwebs   45
Broken across it, and one eye is weeping
From a twig's having lashed across it open.
I'd like to get away from earth awhile
And then come back to it and begin over.
May no fate willfully misunderstand me   50
And half grant what I wish and snatch me away
Not to return. Earth's the right place for love:
I don't know where it's likely to go better.
I'd like to go by climbing a birch tree,
And climb black branches up a snow-white trunk   55
Toward heaven, till the tree could bear no more,
But dipped its top and set me down again.
That would be good both going and coming back.
One could do worse than be a swinger of birches.

122

PEA BRUSH

I walked down alone Sunday after church
    To the place where John has been cutting trees,
To see for myself about the birch
    He said I could have to bush my peas.

The sun in the new-cut narrow gap   5
    Was hot enough for the first of May,
And stifling hot with the odor of sap
    From stumps still bleeding their life away.

The frogs that were peeping a thousand shrill
    Wherever the ground was low and wet,   10
The minute they heard my step went still
    To watch me and see what I came to get.

Birch boughs enough piled everywhere!—
    All fresh and sound from the recent ax.
Time someone came with cart and pair   15
    And got them off the wild flowers' backs.

They might be good for garden things
    To curl a little finger round,
The same as you seize cat's-cradle strings,
    And lift themselves up off the ground.   20

Small good to anything growing wild,
    They were crooking many a trillium
That had budded before the boughs were piled
    And since it was coming up had to come.

PUTTING IN THE SEED

You come to fetch me from my work tonight
When supper's on the table, and we'll see

123

If I can leave off burying the white
Soft petals fallen from the apple tree
(Soft petals, yes, but not so barren quite,   5
Mingled with these, smooth bean and wrinkled pea),
And go along with you ere you lose sight
Of what you came for and become like me,
Slave to a springtime passion for the earth.
How Love burns through the Putting in the Seed   10
On through the watching for that early birth
When, just as the soil tarnishes with weed,
The sturdy seedling with arched body comes
Shouldering its way and shedding the earth crumbs.

A TIME TO TALK

When a friend calls to me from the road
And slows his horse to a meaning walk,
I don't stand still and look around
On all the hills I haven't hoed,
And shout from where I am, "What is it?"   5
No, not as there is a time to talk.
I thrust my hoe in the mellow ground,
Blade-end up and five feet tall,
And plod: I go up to the stone wall
For a friendly visit.   10

THE COW IN APPLE TIME

Something inspires the only cow of late
To make no more of a wall than an open gate,
And think no more of wall-builders than fools.
Her face is flecked with pomace and she drools
A cider syrup. Having tasted fruit,   5

124

She scorns a pasture withering to the root.
She runs from tree to tree where lie and sweeten
The windfalls spiked with stubble and worm-eaten.
She leaves them bitten when she has to fly.
She bellows on a knoll against the sky.   10
Her udder shrivels and the milk goes dry.

AN ENCOUNTER

Once on the kind of day called "weather breeder,"
When the heat slowly hazes and the sun
By its own power seems to be undone,
I was half boring through, half climbing through
A swamp of cedar. Choked with oil of cedar   5
And scurf of plants, and weary and overheated,
And sorry I ever left the road I knew,
I paused and rested on a sort of hook
That had me by the coat as good as seated,
And since there was no other way to look,   10
Looked up toward heaven, and there against the blue,
Stood over me a resurrected tree,
A tree that had been down and raised again—
A barkless specter. He had halted too,
As if for fear of treading upon me.   15
I saw the strange position of his hands—
Up at his shoulders, dragging yellow strands
Of wire with something in it from men to men.
"You here?" I said. "Where aren't you nowadays?
And what's the news you carry—if you know?   20
And tell me where you're off for—Montreal?
Me? I'm not off for anywhere at all.
Sometimes I wander out of beaten ways
Half looking for the orchid Calypso."

125

RANGE-FINDING

The battle rent a cobweb diamond-strung
And cut a flower beside a groundbird's nest
Before it stained a single human breast.
The stricken flower bent double and so hung.
And still the bird revisited her young.   5
A butterfly its fall had dispossessed,
A moment sought in air his flower of rest,
Then lightly stooped to it and fluttering clung.
On the bare upland pasture there had spread
O'ernight 'twixt mullein stalks a wheel of thread   10
And straining cables wet with silver dew.
A sudden passing bullet shook it dry.
The indwelling spider ran to greet the fly,
But finding nothing, sullenly withdrew.

THE HILL WIFE

I. LONELINESS

Her Word

One ought not to have to care
   So much as you and I
Care when the birds come round the house
   To seem to say good-by;

Or care so much when they come back   5
   With whatever it is they sing;
The truth being we are as much
   Too glad for the one thing

As we are too sad for the other here—
   With birds that fill their breasts   10

126

But with each other and themselves
And their built or driven nests.

II. HOUSE FEAR

Always—I tell you this they learned—
Always at night when they returned
To the lonely house from far away,
To lamps unlighted and fire gone gray,
They learned to rattle the lock and key   5
To give whatever might chance to be,
Warning and time to be off in flight:
And preferring the out- to the indoor night,
They learned to leave the house door wide
Until they had lit the lamp inside.   10

III. THE SMILE

Her Word

I didn't like the way he went away.
That smile! It never came of being gay.
Still he smiled—did you see him?—I was sure!
Perhaps because we gave him only bread
And the wretch knew from that that we were poor.   5
Perhaps because he let us give instead
Of seizing from us as he might have seized.
Perhaps he mocked at us for being wed,
Or being very young (and he was pleased
To have a vision of us old and dead).   10
I wonder how far down the road he's got.
He's watching from the woods as like as not.

IV.   THE OFT-REPEATED DREAM

She had no saying dark enough
   For the dark pine that kept
Forever trying the window latch
   Of the room where they slept.

The tireless but ineffectual hands   5
   That with every futile pass
Made the great tree seem as a little bird
   Before the mystery of glass!

It never had been inside the room,
   And only one of the two   10
Was afraid in an oft-repeated dream
   Of what the tree might do.

V.   THE IMPULSE

It was too lonely for her there,
   And too wild,
And since there were but two of them,
   And no child,

And work was little in the house,   5
   She was free,
And followed where he furrowed field,
   Or felled tree.

She rested on a log and tossed
   The fresh chips,   10
With a song only to herself
   On her lips.

And once she went to break a bough
    Of black alder.
She strayed so far she scarcely heard   15
    When he called her—

And didn't answer—didn't speak—
    Or return.
She stood, and then she ran and hid
    In the fern.   20

He never found her, though he looked
    Everywhere,
And he asked at her mother's house
    Was she there.

Sudden and swift and light as that   25
    The ties gave,
And he learned of finalities
    Besides the grave.

THE BONFIRE

"Oh, let's go up the hill and scare ourselves,
As reckless as the best of them tonight,
By setting fire to all the brush we piled
With pitchy hands to wait for rain or snow.
Oh, let's not wait for rain to make it safe.   5
The pile is ours: we dragged it bough on bough
Down dark converging paths between the pines.
Let's not care what we do with it tonight.
Divide it? No! But burn it as one pile
The way we piled it. And let's be the talk   10
Of people brought to windows by a light
Thrown from somewhere against their wallpaper.

129

Rouse them all, both the free and not so free
With saying what they'd like to do to us
For what they'd better wait till we have done.   15
Let's all but bring to life this old volcano,
If that is what the mountain ever was—
And scare ourselves. Let wild fire loose we will——"

"And scare you too?" the children said together.

"Why wouldn't it scare me to have a fire   20
Begin in smudge with ropy smoke, and know
That still, if I repent, I may recall it,
But in a moment not: a little spurt
Of burning fatness, and then nothing but
The fire itself can put it out, and that   25
By burning out, and before it burns out
It will have roared first and mixed sparks with stars,
And sweeping round it with a flaming sword,
Made the dim trees stand back in wider circle—
Done so much and I know not how much more   30
I mean it shall not do if I can bind it.
Well if it doesn't with its draft bring on
A wind to blow in earnest from some quarter,
As once it did with me upon an April.
The breezes were so spent with winter blowing   35
They seemed to fail the bluebirds under them
Short of the perch their languid flight was toward;
And my flame made a pinnacle to heaven
As I walked once around it in possession.
But the wind out-of-doors—you know the saying.   40
There came a gust. (You used to think the trees
Made wind by fanning, since you never knew
It blow but that you saw the trees in motion.)
Something or someone watching made that gust.

It put the flame tip-down and dabbed the grass 45
Of over-winter with the least tip-touch
Your tongue gives salt or sugar in your hand.
The place it reached to blackened instantly.
The black was almost all there was by daylight,
That and the merest curl of cigarette smoke— 50
And a flame slender as the hepaticas,
Bloodroot, and violets so soon to be now.
But the black spread like black death on the ground,
And I think the sky darkened with a cloud
Like winter and evening coming on together. 55
There were enough things to be thought of then.
Where the field stretches toward the north
And setting sun to Hyla brook, I gave it
To flames without twice thinking, where it verges
Upon the road, to flames too, though in fear 60
They might find fuel there, in withered brake,
Grass its full length, old silver goldenrod,
And alder and grape vine entanglement,
To leap the dusty deadline. For my own
I took what front there was beside. I knelt 65
And thrust hands in and held my face away.
Fight such a fire by rubbing not by beating.
A board is the best weapon if you have it.
I had my coat. And oh, I knew, I knew,
And said out loud, I couldn't bide the smother 70
And heat so close in; but the thought of all
The woods and town on fire by me, and all
The town turned out to fight for me—that held me.
I trusted the brook barrier, but feared
The road would fail; and on that side the fire 75
Died not without a noise of crackling wood—
Of something more than tinder-grass and weed—

131

That brought me to my feet to hold it back
By leaning back myself, as if the reins
Were round my neck and I was at the plow.   80
I won! But I'm sure no one ever spread
Another color over a tenth the space
That I spread coal-black over in the time
It took me. Neighbors coming home from town
Couldn't believe that so much black had come there   85
While they had backs turned, that it hadn't been there
When they had passed an hour or so before
Going the other way and they not seen it.
They looked about for someone to have done it.
But there was no one. I was somewhere wondering   90
Where all my weariness had gone and why
I walked so light on air in heavy shoes
In spite of a scorched Fourth-of-July feeling.
Why wouldn't I be scared remembering that?"

"If it scares you, what will it do to us?"   95

"Scare you. But if you shrink from being scared,
What would you say to war if it should come?
That's what for reasons I should like to know—
If you can comfort me by any answer."

"Oh, but war's not for children—it's for men."   100

"Now we are digging almost down to China.
My dears, my dears, you thought that—we all thought it.
So your mistake was ours. Haven't you heard, though,
About the ships where war has found them out
At sea, about the towns where war has come   105
Through opening clouds at night with droning speed
Further o'erhead than all but stars and angels—
And children in the ships and in the towns?

132

Haven't you heard what we have lived to learn?
Nothing so new—something we had forgotten: 110
War is for everyone, for children too.
I wasn't going to tell you and I mustn't.
The best way is to come uphill with me
And have our fire and laugh and be afraid."

A GIRL'S GARDEN

A neighbor of mine in the village
   Likes to tell how one spring
When she was a girl on the farm, she did
   A childlike thing.

One day she asked her father   5
   To give her a garden plot
To plant and tend and reap herself,
   And he said, "Why not?"

In casting about for a corner
   He thought of an idle bit   10
Of walled-off ground where a shop had stood,
   And he said, "Just it."

And he said, "That ought to make you
   An ideal one-girl farm,
And give you a chance to put some strength   15
   On your slim-jim arm."

It was not enough of a garden,
   Her father said, to plow;
So she had to work it all by hand,
   But she don't mind now.   20

133

She wheeled the dung in the wheelbarrow
  Along a stretch of road;
But she always ran away and left
  Her not-nice load,

And hid from anyone passing.   25
  And then she begged the seed.
She says she thinks she planted one
  Of all things but weed.

A hill each of potatoes,
  Radishes, lettuce, peas,   30
Tomatoes, beets, beans, pumpkins, corn,
  And even fruit trees.

And yes, she has long mistrusted
  That a cider-apple tree
In bearing there today is hers,   35
  Or at least may be.

Her crop was a miscellany
  When all was said and done,
A little bit of everything,
  A great deal of none.   40

Now when she sees in the village
  How village things go,
Just when it seems to come in right,
  She says, "*I* know!

"It's as when I was a farmer. . . ."   45
  Oh, never by way of advice!
And she never sins by telling the tale
  To the same person twice.

134

LOCKED OUT

As told to a child

When we locked up the house at night,
We always locked the flowers outside
And cut them off from window light.
The time I dreamed the door was tried
And brushed with buttons upon sleeves,   5
The flowers were out there with the thieves.
Yet nobody molested them!
We did find one nasturtium
Upon the steps with bitten stem.
I may have been to blame for that: 10
I always thought it must have been
Some flower I played with as I sat
At dusk to watch the moon down early.

THE LAST WORD OF A BLUEBIRD

As told to a child

As I went out a Crow
In a low voice said, "Oh,
I was looking for you.
How do you do?
I just came to tell you   5
To tell Lesley (will you?)
That her little Bluebird
Wanted me to bring word
That the north wind last night
That made the stars bright   10
And made ice on the trough
Almost made him cough
His tail feathers off.

135

He just had to fly!
But he sent her Good-by,   15
And said to be good,
And wear her red hood,
And look for skunk tracks
In the snow with an ax—
And do everything!   20
And perhaps in the spring
He would come back and sing."

"OUT, OUT—"

The buzz saw snarled and rattled in the yard
And made dust and dropped stove-length sticks of wood,
Sweet-scented stuff when the breeze drew across it.
And from there those that lifted eyes could count
Five mountain ranges one behind the other   5
Under the sunset far into Vermont.
And the saw snarled and rattled, snarled and rattled,
As it ran light, or had to bear a load.
And nothing happened: day was all but done.
Call it a day, I wish they might have said   10
To please the boy by giving him the half hour
That a boy counts so much when saved from work.
His sister stood beside them in her apron
To tell them "Supper." At the word, the saw,
As if to prove saws knew what supper meant,   15
Leaped out at the boy's hand, or seemed to leap—
He must have given the hand. However it was,
Neither refused the meeting. But the hand!
The boy's first outcry was a rueful laugh,
As he swung toward them holding up the hand,   20

Half in appeal, but half as if to keep
The life from spilling. Then the boy saw all—
Since he was old enough to know, big boy
Doing a man's work, though a child at heart—
He saw all spoiled. "Don't let him cut my hand off—   25
The doctor, when he comes. Don't let him, sister!"
So. But the hand was gone already.
The doctor put him in the dark of ether.
He lay and puffed his lips out with his breath.
And then—the watcher at his pulse took fright.   30
No one believed. They listened at his heart.
Little—less—nothing!—and that ended it.
No more to build on there. And they, since they
Were not the one dead, turned to their affairs.

BROWN'S DESCENT

Brown lived at such a lofty farm
    That everyone for miles could see
His lantern when he did his chores
    In winter after half-past three.

And many must have seen him make   5
    His wild descent from there one night,
'Cross lots, 'cross walls, 'cross everything,
    Describing rings of lantern-light.

Between the house and barn the gale
    Got him by something he had on   10
And blew him out on the icy crust
    That cased the world, and he was gone!

Walls were all buried, trees were few:
    He saw no stay unless he stove

137

A hole in somewhere with his heel.   15
   But though repeatedly he strove

And stamped and said things to himself,
   And sometimes something seemed to yield,
He gained no foothold, but pursued
   His journey down from field to field.   20

Sometimes he came with arms outspread
   Like wings, revolving in the scene
Upon his longer axis, and
   With no small dignity of mien.

Faster or slower as he chanced,   25
   Sitting or standing as he chose,
According as he feared to risk
   His neck, or thought to spare his clothes.

He never let the lantern drop.
   And some exclaimed who saw afar   30
The figures he described with it,
   "I wonder what those signals are

"Brown makes at such an hour of night!
   He's celebrating something strange.
I wonder if he's sold his farm,   35
   Or been made Master of the Grange."

He reeled, he lurched, he bobbed, he checked;
   He fell and made the lantern rattle
(But saved the light from going out).
   So halfway down he fought the battle,   40

Incredulous of his own bad luck.
   And then becoming reconciled

To everything, he gave it up
    And came down like a coasting child.

"Well—I—be—" that was all he said,   45
    As standing in the river road
He looked back up the slippery slope
    (Two miles it was) to his abode.

Sometimes as an authority
    On motorcars, I'm asked if I   50
Should say our stock was petered out,
    And this is my sincere reply:

Yankees are what they always were.
    Don't think Brown ever gave up hope
Of getting home again because   55
    He couldn't climb that slippery slope;

Or even thought of standing there
    Until the January thaw
Should take the polish off the crust.
    He bowed with grace to natural law,   60

And then went round it on his feet,
    After the manner of our stock;
Not much concerned for those to whom,
    At that particular time o'clock,

It must have looked as if the course   65
    He steered was really straight away
From that which he was headed for—
    Not much concerned for them, I say;

No more so than became a man—
    And politician at odd seasons.   70

139

I've kept Brown standing in the cold
    While I invested him with reasons;

But now he snapped his eyes three times;
    Then shook his lantern, saying, "Ile's
'Bout out!" and took the long way home   75
    By road, a matter of several miles.

THE GUM-GATHERER

There overtook me and drew me in
To his downhill, early-morning stride,
And set me five miles on my road
Better than if he had had me ride,
A man with a swinging bag for load   5
And half the bag wound round his hand.
We talked like barking above the din
Of water we walked along beside.
And for my telling him where I'd been
And where I lived in mountain land   10
To be coming home the way I was,
He told me a little about himself.
He came from higher up in the pass
Where the grist of the new-beginning brooks
Is blocks split off the mountain mass—   15
And hopeless grist enough it looks
Ever to grind to soil for grass.
(The way it is will do for moss.)
There he had built his stolen shack.
It had to be a stolen shack   20
Because of the fears of fire and loss
That trouble the sleep of lumber folk:
Visions of half the world burned black

And the sun shrunken yellow in smoke.
We know who when they come to town   25
Bring berries under the wagon seat,
Or a basket of eggs between their feet;
What this man brought in a cotton sack
Was gum, the gum of the mountain spruce.
He showed me lumps of the scented stuff   30
Like uncut jewels, dull and rough.
It comes to market golden brown;
But turns to pink between the teeth.

I told him this is a pleasant life,
To set your breast to the bark of trees   35
That all your days are dim beneath,
And reaching up with a little knife,
To loose the resin and take it down
And bring it to market when you please.

THE LINE-GANG

Here come the line-gang pioneering by.
They throw a forest down less cut than broken.
They plant dead trees for living, and the dead
They string together with a living thread.
They string an instrument against the sky   5
Wherein words whether beaten out or spoken
Will run as hushed as when they were a thought.
But in no hush they string it: they go past
With shouts afar to pull the cable taut,
To hold it hard until they make it fast,   10
To ease away—they have it. With a laugh,
An oath of towns that set the wild at naught,
They bring the telephone and telegraph.

141

THE VANISHING RED

He is said to have been the last Red Man
In Acton. And the Miller is said to have laughed—
If you like to call such a sound a laugh.
But he gave no one else a laugher's license.
For he turned suddenly grave as if to say,   5
"Whose business—if I take it on myself,
Whose business—but why talk round the barn?—
When it's just that I hold with getting a thing done with."

You can't get back and see it as he saw it.
It's too long a story to go into now.   10
You'd have to have been there and lived it.
Then you wouldn't have looked on it as just a matter
Of who began it between the two races.

Some guttural exclamation of surprise
The Red Man gave in poking about the mill,   15
Over the great big thumping, shuffling millstone,
Disgusted the Miller physically as coming
From one who had no right to be heard from.

"Come, John," he said, "you want to see the wheel pit?"

He took him down below a cramping rafter,   20
And showed him, through a manhole in the floor,
The water in desperate straits like frantic fish,
Salmon and sturgeon, lashing with their tails.
Then he shut down the trap door with a ring in it
That jangled even above the general noise,   25
And came upstairs alone—and gave that laugh,
And said something to a man with a meal sack
That the man with the meal sack didn't catch—then.
Oh, yes, he showed John the wheel pit all right.

142

SNOW

The three stood listening to a fresh access
Of wind that caught against the house a moment,
Gulped snow, and then blew free again—the Coles,
Dressed, but disheveled from some hours of sleep;
Meserve, belittled in the great skin coat he wore.   5

Meserve was first to speak. He pointed backward
Over his shoulder with his pipestem, saying,
"You can just see it glancing off the roof
Making a great scroll upward toward the sky,
Long enough for recording all our names on.—   10
I think I'll just call up my wife and tell her
I'm here—so far—and starting on again.
I'll call her softly so that if she's wise
And gone to sleep, she needn't wake to answer."
Three times he barely stirred the bell, then listened.   15
"Why, Lett, still up? Lett, I'm at Cole's. I'm late.
I called you up to say Good-night from here
Before I went to say Good-morning there.—
I thought I would.—I know, but, Lett—I know—
I could, but what's the sense? The rest won't be   20
So bad.—Give me an hour for it.— Ho, ho,
Three hours to here! But that was all uphill;
The rest is down.—Why no, no, not a wallow:
They kept their heads and took their time to it
Like darlings, both of them. They're in the barn.—   25
My dear, I'm coming just the same. I didn't
Call you to ask you to invite me home.—"
He lingered for some word she wouldn't say,
Said it at last himself, "Good-night," and then,
Getting no answer, closed the telephone.   30

143

The three stood in the lamplight round the table
With lowered eyes a moment till he said,
"I'll just see how the horses are."

                              "Yes, do,"
Both the Coles said together. Mrs. Cole
Added: "You can judge better after seeing.—   35
I want you here with me, Fred.—Leave him here,
Brother Meserve. You know to find your way
Out through the shed."

                         "I guess I know my way.
I guess I know where I can find my name
Carved in the shed to tell me who I am   40
If it don't tell me where I am. I used
To play——"

                    "You tend your horses and come back.—
Fred Cole, you're going to let him!"

                                        "Well, aren't you?
How can you help yourself?"

                              "I called him Brother.
Why did I call him that?"

                             "It's right enough.   45
That's all you ever heard him called round here.
He seems to have lost off his Christian name."

"Christian enough I should call that myself.
He took no notice, did he? Well, at least
I didn't use it out of love of him,   50
The dear knows. I detest the thought of him—
With his ten children under ten years old.
I hate his wretched little Racker Sect,
All's ever I heard of it, which isn't much.
But that's not saying—look, Fred Cole, it's twelve,   55

144

Isn't it, now? He's been here half an hour.
He says he left the village store at nine:
Three hours to do four miles—a mile an hour
Or not much better. Why, it doesn't seem
As if a man could move that slow and move.   60
Try to think what he did with all that time.
And three miles more to go!"

                              "Don't let him go.
Stick to him, Helen. Make him answer you.
That sort of man talks straight-on all his life
From the last thing he said himself, stone deaf   65
To anything anyone else may say.
I should have thought, though, you could make him hear you."

"What is he doing out a night like this?
Why can't he stay at home?"

                              "He had to preach."

"It's no night to be out."

                              "He may be small,   70
He may be good, but one thing's sure, he's tough."

"And strong of stale tobacco."

                              "He'll pull through."

"You only say so. Not another house
Or shelter to put into from this place
To theirs. I'm going to call his wife again."   75

"Wait and he may. Let's see what he will do.
Let's see if he will think of her again.
But then, I doubt he's thinking of himself.
He doesn't look on it as anything."

"He shan't go—there!"

145

"It *is* a night, my dear."   80

"One thing: he didn't drag God into it."

"He don't consider it a case for God."

"You think so, do you? You don't know the kind.
He's getting up a miracle this minute.
Privately—to himself, right now, he's thinking   85
He'll make a case of it if he succeeds,
But keep still if he fails."

                         "Keep still all over.
He'll be dead—dead and buried."

                              "Such a trouble!
Not but I've every reason not to care
What happens to him if it only takes   90
Some of the sanctimonious conceit
Out of one of those pious scalawags."

"Nonsense to that! You want to see him safe."

"You like the runt."

                    "Don't you a little?"

                              "Well,
I don't like what he's doing, which is what   95
You like, and like him for."

                         "Oh, yes you do.
You like your fun as well as anyone;
Only you women have to put these airs on
To impress men. You've got us so ashamed
Of being men we can't look at a good fight   100
Between two boys and not feel bound to stop it.
Let the man freeze an ear or two, I say.—
He's here. I leave him all to you. Go in

And save his life.—All right, come in, Meserve.
Sit down, sit down. How did you find the horses?"   105

"Fine, fine."

          "And ready for some more? My wife here
Says it won't do. You've got to give it up."

"Won't you to please me? Please! If I say **Please**?
Mr. Meserve, I'll leave it to *your* wife.
What *did* your wife say on the telephone?"   110

Meserve seemed to heed nothing but the lamp
Or something not far from it on the table.
By straightening out and lifting a forefinger,
He pointed with his hand from where it lay
Like a white crumpled spider on his knee: 115
"That leaf there in your open book! It moved
Just then, I thought. It's stood erect like that,
There on the table, ever since I came,
Trying to turn itself backward or forward,
I've had my eye on it to make out which: 120
If forward, then it's with a friend's impatience—
You see I know—to get you on to things
It wants to see how you will take; if backward,
It's from regret for something you have passed
And failed to see the good of. Never mind,   125
Things must expect to come in front of us
A many times—I don't say just how many—
That varies with the things—before we see them.
One of the lies would make it out that nothing
Ever presents itself before us twice.   130
Where would we be at last if that were so?
Our very life depends on everything's
Recurring till we answer from within.

147

The thousandth time may prove the charm.—That leaf!
It can't turn either way. It needs the wind's help.   135
But the wind didn't move it if it moved.
It moved itself. The wind's at naught in here.
It couldn't stir so sensitively poised
A thing as that. It couldn't reach the lamp
To get a puff of black smoke from the flame,   140
Or blow a rumple in the collie's coat.
You make a little foursquare block of air,
Quiet and light and warm, in spite of all
The illimitable dark and cold and storm,
And by so doing give these three, lamp, dog,   145
And book-leaf, that keep near you, their repose;
Though for all anyone can tell, repose
May be the thing you haven't, yet you give it.
So false it is that what we haven't we can't give;
So false, that what we always say is true.   150
I'll have to turn the leaf if no one else will.
It won't lie down. Then let it stand. Who cares?"

"I shouldn't want to hurry you, Meserve,
But if you're going—say you'll stay, you know.
But let me raise this curtain on a scene,   155
And show you how it's piling up against you.
You see the snow-white through the white of frost?
Ask Helen how far up the sash it's climbed
Since last we read the gauge."

                                  "It looks as if
Some pallid thing had squashed its features flat   160
And its eyes shut with overeagerness
To see what people found so interesting
In one another, and had gone to sleep
Of its own stupid lack of understanding,

148

Or broken its white neck of mushroom stuff   165
Short off, and died against the windowpane."

"Brother Meserve, take care, you'll scare yourself
More than you will us with such nightmare talk.
It's you it matters to, because it's you
Who have to go out into it alone."   170

"Let him talk, Helen, and perhaps he'll stay."

"Before you drop the curtain—I'm reminded:
You recollect the boy who came out here
To breathe the air one winter—had a room
Down at the Averys'? Well, one sunny morning   175
After a downy storm, he passed our place
And found me banking up the house with snow.
And I was burrowing in deep for warmth,
Piling it well above the windowsills.
The snow against the window caught his eye.   180
'Hey, that's a pretty thought'—those were his words—
'So you can think it's six feet deep outside,
While you sit warm and read up balanced rations.
You can't get too much winter in the winter.'
Those were his words. And he went home and all   185
But banked the daylight out of Avery's windows.
Now you and I would go to no such length.
At the same time you can't deny it makes
It not a mite worse, sitting here, we three,
Playing our fancy, to have the snow-line run   190
So high across the pane outside. There where
There is a sort of tunnel in the frost—
More like a tunnel than a hole—way down
At the far end of it you see a stir
And quiver like the frayed edge of the drift   195

149

Blown in the wind. I *like* that—I like *that.*
Well, now I leave you, people."

                          "Come, Meserve,
We thought you were deciding not to go—
The ways you found to say the praise of comfort
And being where you are. You want to stay."   200

"I'll own it's cold for such a fall of snow.
This house is frozen brittle, all except
This room you sit in. If you think the wind
Sounds further off, it's not because it's dying;
You're further under in the snow—that's all—   205
And feel it less. Hear the soft bombs of dust
It bursts against us at the chimney mouth,
And at the eaves. I like it from inside
More than I shall out in it. But the horses
Are rested and it's time to say Good-night,   210
And let you get to bed again. Good-night,
Sorry I had to break in on your sleep."

"Lucky for you you did. Lucky for you
You had us for a halfway station
To stop at. If you were the kind of man   215
Paid heed to women, you'd take my advice
And for your family's sake stay where you are.
But what good is my saying it over and over?
You've done more than you had a right to think
You could do—*now.* You know the risk you take   220
In going on."

               "Our snowstorms as a rule
Aren't looked on as man-killers, and although
I'd rather be the beast that sleeps the sleep
Under it all, his door sealed up and lost,

150

Than the man fighting it to keep above it,   225
Yet think of the small birds at roost and not
In nests. Shall I be counted less than they are?
Their bulk in water would be frozen rock
In no time out tonight. And yet tomorrow
They will come budding boughs from tree to tree,   230
Flirting their wings and saying Chickadee,
As if not knowing what you meant by the word storm."

"But why, when no one wants you to, go on?
Your wife—she doesn't want you to. We don't,
And you yourself don't want to. Who else is there?"   235

"Save us from being cornered by a woman.
Well, there's—" She told Fred afterward that in
The pause right there, she thought the dreaded word
Was coming, "God." But no, he only said,
"Well, there's—the storm. That says I must go on.   240
That wants me as a war might if it came.
Ask any man."

       He threw her that as something
To last her till he got outside the door.
He had Cole with him to the barn to see him off.
When Cole returned he found his wife still standing   245
Beside the table, near the open book,
Not reading it.

       "Well, what kind of a man
Do you call that?" she said.

       "He had the gift
Of words, or is it tongues I ought to say?"

"Was ever such a man for seeing likeness?"   250

"Or disregarding people's civil questions—

151

What? We've found out in one hour more about him
Than we had seeing him pass by in the road
A thousand times. If that's the way he preaches!
You didn't think you'd keep him after all.   255
Oh, I'm not blaming you. He didn't leave you
Much say in the matter, and I'm just as glad
We're not in for a night of him. No sleep
If he had stayed. The least thing set him going.
It's quiet as an empty church without him."   260

"But how much better off are we as it is?
We'll have to sit here till we know he's safe."

"Yes, I suppose you'll want to, but I shouldn't.
He knows what he can do, or he wouldn't try.
Get into bed I say, and get some rest.   265
He won't come back, and if he telephones,
It won't be for an hour or two."

                                    "Well then—
We can't be any help by sitting here
And living his fight through with him, I suppose."

                    *   *   *

Cole had been telephoning in the dark.   270
Mrs. Cole's voice came from an inner room:
"Did she call you or you call her?"

                                    "She me.
You'd better dress: you won't go back to bed.
We must have been asleep: it's three and after."

"Had she been ringing long? I'll get my wrapper.   275
I want to speak to her."

                    "All she said was,
He hadn't come and had he really started."

152

"She knew he had, poor thing, two hours ago."

"He had the shovel. He'll have made a fight."

"Why did I ever let him leave this house!"   280

"Don't begin that. You did the best you could
To keep him—though perhaps you didn't quite
Conceal a wish to see him show the spunk
To disobey you. Much his wife'll thank you."

"Fred, after all I said! You shan't make out   285
That it was any way but what it was.
Did she let on by any word she said
She didn't thank me?"

               "When I told her 'Gone,'
'Well then,' she said, and 'Well then'—like a threat.
And then her voice came scraping slow: 'Oh, you,   290
Why did you let him go?' "

               "Asked why we let him?
You let me there. I'll ask her why she let him.
She didn't dare to speak when he was here.
Their number's—twenty-one?—The thing won't work.
Someone's receiver's down. The handle stumbles.   295
The stubborn thing, the way it jars your arm!—
It's theirs. She's dropped it from her hand and gone."

"Try speaking. Say 'Hello!' "

               "Hello. Hello."

"What do you hear?"

               "I hear an empty room—
You know—it sounds that way. And yes, I hear—   300
I think I hear a clock—and windows rattling.
No step, though. If she's there she's sitting down."

153

"Shout, she may hear you."

             "Shouting is no good."

"Keep speaking, then."

          "Hello. Hello. Hello.—
You don't suppose?—she wouldn't go outdoors?"   305

"I'm half afraid that's just what she might do."

"And leave the children?"

            "Wait and call again.
You can't hear whether she has left the door
Wide open and the wind's blown out the lamp
And the fire's died and the room's dark and cold?"   310

"One of two things, either she's gone to bed
Or gone outdoors."

        "In which case both are lost.
Do you know what she's like? Have you ever met her?
It's strange she doesn't want to speak to us."

"Fred, see if you can hear what I hear. Come."   315

"A clock maybe."

       "Don't you hear something else?"

"Not talking."

     "No."

       "Why, yes, I hear—what is it?"

"What do you say it is?"

        "A baby's crying!
Frantic it sounds, though muffled and far off.
Its mother wouldn't let it cry like that,   320
Not if she's there."

154

"What do you make of it?"

"There's only one thing possible to make,
That is, assuming—that she has gone out.
Of course she hasn't, though." They both sat down
Helpless. "There's nothing we can do till morning."   325

"Fred, I shan't let you think of going out."

"Hold on." The double bell began to chirp.
They started up. Fred took the telephone.
"Hello, Meserve. You're there, then!—and your wife?
Good! Why I asked—she didn't seem to answer.—   330
He says she went to let him in the barn.—
We're glad. Oh, say no more about it, man.
Drop in and see us when you're passing."

                                        "Well,
She has him, then, though what she wants him for
I *don't* see."

                        "Possibly not for herself.   335
Maybe she only wants him for the children."

"The whole to-do seems to have been for nothing.
What spoiled our night was to him just his fun.
What did he come in for?—to talk and visit?
Thought he'd just call to tell us it was snowing.   340
If he thinks he is going to make our house
A halfway coffee house 'twixt town and nowhere——"

"I thought you'd feel you'd been too much concerned."

"You think you haven't been concerned yourself."

"If you mean he was inconsiderate   345
To rout us out to think for him at midnight
And then take our advice no more than nothing,

155

Why, I agree with you. But let's forgive him.
We've had a share in one night of his life.
What'll you bet he ever calls again?"

THE SOUND OF TREES

I wonder about the trees.
Why do we wish to bear
Forever the noise of these
More than another noise
So close to our dwelling place?   5
We suffer them by the day
Till we lose all measure of pace,
And fixity in our joys,
And acquire a listening air.
They are that that talks of going   10
But never gets away;
And that talks no less for knowing,
As it grows wiser and older,
That now it means to stay.
My feet tug at the floor   15
And my head sways to my shoulder
Sometimes when I watch trees sway,
From the window or the door.
I shall set forth for somewhere,
I shall make the reckless choice   20
Some day when they are in voice
And tossing so as to scare
The white clouds over them on.
I shall have less to say,
But I shall be gone.   25

New Hampshire

: 1923 :

NEW HAMPSHIRE

I met a lady from the South who said
(You won't believe she said it, but she said it):
"None of my family ever worked, or had
A thing to sell." I don't suppose the work
Much matters. You may work for all of me.   5
I've seen the time I've had to work myself.
The having anything to sell is what
Is the disgrace in man or state or nation.

I met a traveler from Arkansas
Who boasted of his state as beautiful   10
For diamonds and apples. "Diamonds
And apples in commercial quantities?"
I asked him, on my guard. "Oh, yes," he answered,
Off his. The time was evening in the Pullman.
"I see the porter's made your bed," I told him.   15

I met a Californian who would
Talk California—a state so blessed,
He said, in climate, none had ever died there
A natural death, and Vigilance Committees
Had had to organize to stock the graveyards   20
And vindicate the state's humanity.
"Just the way Stefansson runs on," I murmured,
"About the British Arctic. That's what comes
Of being in the market with a climate."

I met a poet from another state,   25
A zealot full of fluid inspiration,
Who in the name of fluid inspiration,

159

But in the best style of bad salesmanship,
Angrily tried to make me write a protest
(In verse I think) against the Volstead Act.   30
He didn't even offer me a drink
Until I asked for one to steady *him*.
This is called having an idea to sell.

It never could have happened in New Hampshire.

The only person really soiled with trade   35
I ever stumbled on in old New Hampshire
Was someone who had just come back ashamed
From selling things in California.
He'd built a noble mansard roof with balls
On turrets, like Constantinople, deep   40
In woods some ten miles from a railroad station,
As if to put forever out of mind
The hope of being, as we say, received.
I found him standing at the close of day
Inside the threshold of his open barn,   45
Like a lone actor on a gloomy stage—
And recognized him, through the iron gray
In which his face was muffled to the eyes,
As an old boyhood friend, and once indeed
A drover with me on the road to Brighton.   50
His farm was "grounds," and not a farm at all;
His house among the local sheds and shanties
Rose like a factor's at a trading station.
And he was rich, and I was still a rascal.
I couldn't keep from asking impolitely,   55
Where had he been and what had he been doing?
How did he get so? (Rich was understood.)
In dealing in "old rags" in San Francisco.
Oh, it was terrible as well could be.

We both of us turned over in our graves.   60

Just specimens is all New Hampshire has,
One each of everything as in a showcase,
Which naturally she doesn't care to sell.

She had one President. (Pronounce him Purse,
And make the most of it for better or worse.   65
He's your one chance to score against the state.)
She had one Daniel Webster. He was all
The Daniel Webster ever was or shall be.
She had the Dartmouth needed to produce him.

I call her old. She has one family   70
Whose claim is good to being settled here
Before the era of colonization,
And before that of exploration even.
John Smith remarked them as he coasted by,
Dangling their legs and fishing off a wharf   75
At the Isles of Shoals, and satisfied himself
They weren't Red Indians but veritable
Pre-primitives of the white race, dawn people,
Like those who furnished Adam's sons with wives;
However uninnocent they may have been   80
In being there so early in our history.
They'd been there then a hundred years or more.
Pity he didn't ask what they were up to
At that date with a wharf already built,
And take their name. They've since told me their name—
Today an honored one in Nottingham.
As for what they were up to more than fishing—
Suppose they weren't behaving Puritanly,
The hour had not yet struck for being good,
Mankind had not yet gone on the Sabbatical.   90

161

It became an explorer of the deep
Not to explore too deep in others' business.

Did you but know of him, New Hampshire has
One real reformer who would change the world
So it would be accepted by two classes,   95
Artists the minute they set up as artists,
Before, that is, they are themselves accepted,
And boys the minute they get out of college.
I can't help thinking those are tests to go by.

And she has one I don't know what to call him,   100
Who comes from Philadelphia every year
With a great flock of chickens of rare breeds
He wants to give the educational
Advantages of growing almost wild
Under the watchful eye of hawk and eagle—   105
Dorkings because they're spoken of by Chaucer,
Sussex because they're spoken of by Herrick.

She has a touch of gold. New Hampshire gold—
You may have heard of it. I had a farm
Offered me not long since up Berlin way   110
With a mine on it that was worked for gold;
But not gold in commercial quantities,
Just enough gold to make the engagement rings
And marriage rings of those who owned the farm.
What gold more innocent could one have asked for?   115
One of my children ranging after rocks
Lately brought home from Andover or Canaan
A specimen of beryl with a trace
Of radium. I know with radium
The trace would have to be the merest trace   120
To be below the threshold of commercial;

162

But trust New Hampshire not to have enough
Of radium or anything to sell.

A specimen of everything, I said.
She has one witch—old style. She lives in Colebrook.   125
(The only other witch I ever met
Was lately at a cut-glass dinner in Boston.
There were four candles and four people present.
The witch was young, and beautiful (new style),
And open-minded. She was free to question   130
Her gift for reading letters locked in boxes.
Why was it so much greater when the boxes
Were metal than it was when they were wooden?
It made the world seem so mysterious.
The S'ciety for Psychical Research   135
Was cognizant. Her husband was worth millions.
I think he owned some shares in Harvard College.)

New Hampshire *used* to have at Salem
A company we called the White Corpuscles,
Whose duty was at any hour of night   140
To rush in sheets and fool's caps where they smelled
A thing the least bit doubtfully perscented
And give someone the Skipper Ireson's Ride.

One each of everything as in a showcase.

More than enough land for a specimen   145
You'll say she has, but there there enters in
Something else to protect her from herself.
There quality makes up for quantity.
Not even New Hampshire farms are much for sale.
The farm I made my home on in the mountains   150
I had to take by force rather than buy.

163

I caught the owner outdoors by himself
Raking up after winter, and I said,
"I'm going to put you off this farm: I want it."
"Where are you going to put me? In the road?"   155
"I'm going to put you on the farm next to it."
"Why won't the farm next to it do for you?"
"I like this better." It was really better.

Apples? New Hampshire has them, but unsprayed,
With no suspicion in stem end or blossom end   160
Of vitriol or arsenate of lead,
And so not good for anything but cider.
Her unpruned grapes are flung like lariats
Far up the birches out of reach of man.

A state producing precious metals, stones,   165
And—writing; none of these except perhaps
The precious literature in quantity
Or quality to worry the producer
About disposing of it. Do you know,
Considering the market, there are more   170
Poems produced than any other thing?
No wonder poets sometimes have to *seem*
So much more businesslike than businessmen.
Their wares are so much harder to get rid of.

She's one of the two best states in the Union.   175
Vermont's the other. And the two have been
Yokefellows in the sap yoke from of old
In many Marches. And they lie like wedges,
Thick end to thin end and thin end to thick end,
And are a figure of the way the strong   180
Of mind and strong of arm should fit together,
One thick where one is thin and vice versa.

164

New Hampshire raises the Connecticut
In a trout hatchery near Canada,
But soon divides the river with Vermont.   185
Both are delightful states for their absurdly
Small towns—Lost Nation, Bungey, Muddy Boo,
Poplin, Still Corners (so called not because
The place is silent all day long, nor yet
Because it boasts a whisky still—because   190
It set out once to be a city and still
Is only corners, crossroads in a wood).
And I remember one whose name appeared
Between the pictures on a movie screen
Election night once in Franconia,   195
When everything had gone Republican
And Democrats were sore in need of comfort:
Easton goes Democratic, Wilson 4
Hughes 2. And everybody to the saddest
Laughed the loud laugh the big laugh at the little.   200
New York (five million) laughs at Manchester,
Manchester (sixty or seventy thousand) laughs
At Littleton (four thousand), Littleton
Laughs at Franconia (seven hundred), and
Franconia laughs, I fear—did laugh that night—   205
At Easton. What has Easton left to laugh at,
And like the actress exclaim "Oh, my God" at?
There's Bungey; and for Bungey there are towns,
Whole townships named but without population.

Anything I can say about New Hampshire   210
Will serve almost as well about Vermont,
Excepting that they differ in their mountains.
The Vermont mountains stretch extended straight;
New Hampshire mountains curl up in a coil.

165

I had been coming to New Hampshire mountains.   215
And here I am and what am I to say?
Here first my theme becomes embarrassing.
Emerson said, "The God who made New Hampshire
Taunted the lofty land with little men."
Another Massachusetts poet said,   220
"I go no more to summer in New Hampshire.
I've given up my summer place in Dublin."
But when I asked to know what ailed New Hampshire,
She said she couldn't stand the people in it,
The little men (it's Massachusetts speaking).   225
And when I asked to know what ailed the people,
She said, "Go read your own books and find out."
I may as well confess myself the author
Of several books against the world in general.
To take them as against a special state   230
Or even nation's to restrict my meaning.
I'm what is called a sensibilitist,
Or otherwise an environmentalist.
I refuse to adapt myself a mite
To any change from hot to cold, from wet   235
To dry, from poor to rich, or back again.
I make a virtue of my suffering
From nearly everything that goes on round me.
In other words, I know wherever I am,
Being the creature of literature I am,   240
I shall not lack for pain to keep me awake.
Kit Marlowe taught me how to say my prayers:
"Why, this is Hell, nor am I out of it."
Samoa, Russia, Ireland I complain of,
No less than England, France, and Italy.   245
Because I wrote my novels in New Hampshire
Is no proof that I aimed them at New Hampshire.

When I left Massachusetts years ago
Between two days, the reason why I sought
New Hampshire, not Connecticut,   250
Rhode Island, New York, or Vermont was this:
Where I was living then, New Hampshire offered
The nearest boundary to escape across.
I hadn't an illusion in my handbag
About the people being better there   255
Than those I left behind. I thought they weren't.
I thought they couldn't be. And yet they were.
I'd sure had no such friends in Massachusetts
As Hall of Windham, Gay of Atkinson,
Bartlett of Raymond (now of Colorado),   260
Harris of Derry, and Lynch of Bethlehem.

The glorious bards of Massachusetts seem
To want to make New Hampshire people over.
They taunt the lofty land with little men.
I don't know what to say about the people.   265
For art's sake one could almost wish them worse
Rather than better. How are we to write
The Russian novel in America
As long as life goes so unterribly?
There is the pinch from which our only outcry   270
In literature to date is heard to come.
We get what little misery we can
Out of not having cause for misery.
It makes the guild of novel writers sick
To be expected to be Dostoievskis   275
On nothing worse than too much luck and comfort.
This is not sorrow, though; it's just the vapors,
And recognized as such in Russia itself
Under the new regime, and so forbidden.

If well it is with Russia, then feel free   280
To say so or be stood against the wall
And shot. It's Pollyanna now or death.
This, then, is the new freedom we hear tell of;
And very sensible. No state can build
A literature that shall at once be sound   285
And sad on a foundation of well-being.

To show the level of intelligence
Among us: it was just a Warren farmer
Whose horse had pulled him short up in the road
By me, a stranger. This is what he said,   290
From nothing but embarrassment and want
Of anything more sociable to say:
"You hear those hound dogs sing on Moosilauke?
Well, they remind me of the hue and cry
We've heard against the Mid-Victorians   295
And never rightly understood till Bryan
Retired from politics and joined the chorus.
The matter with the Mid-Victorians
Seems to have been a man named John L. Darwin."
"Go 'long," I said to him, he to his horse.   300

I knew a man who failing as a farmer
Burned down his farmhouse for the fire insurance,
And spent the proceeds on a telescope
To satisfy a lifelong curiosity
About our place among the infinities.   305
And how was that for otherworldliness?

If I must choose which I would elevate—
The people or the already lofty mountains,
I'd elevate the already lofty mountains.
The only fault I find with old New Hampshire   310

168

Is that her mountains aren't quite high enough.
I was not always so; I've come to be so.
How, to my sorrow, how have I attained
A height from which to look down critical
On mountains? What has given me assurance   315
To say what height becomes New Hampshire mountains,
Or any mountains? Can it be some strength
I feel, as of an earthquake in my back,
To heave them higher to the morning star?
Can it be foreign travel in the Alps?   320
Or having seen and credited a moment
The solid molding of vast peaks of cloud
Behind the pitiful reality
Of Lincoln, Lafayette, and Liberty?
Or some such sense as says how high shall jet   325
The fountain in proportion to the basin?
No, none of these has raised me to my throne
Of intellectual dissatisfaction,
But the sad accident of having seen
Our actual mountains given in a map   330
Of early times as twice the height they are—
Ten thousand feet instead of only five—
Which shows how sad an accident may be.
Five thousand is no longer high enough.
Whereas I never had a good idea   335
About improving people in the world,
Here I am overfertile in suggestion,
And cannot rest from planning day or night
How high I'd thrust the peaks in summer snow
To tap the upper sky and draw a flow   340
Of frosty night air on the vale below
Down from the stars to freeze the dew as starry.

The more the sensibilitist I am
The more I seem to want my mountains wild;
The way the wiry gang-boss liked the logjam.   345
After he'd picked the lock and got it started,
He dodged a log that lifted like an arm
Against the sky to break his back for him,
Then came in dancing, skipping with his life
Across the roar and chaos, and the words   350
We saw him say along the zigzag journey
Were doubtless as the words we heard him say
On coming nearer: "Wasn't she an *i*-deal
Son-of-a-bitch? You bet she was an *i*-deal."

For all her mountains fall a little short,   355
Her people not quite short enough for Art,
She's still New Hampshire, a most restful state.

Lately in converse with a New York alec
About the new school of the pseudo-phallic,
I found myself in a close corner where   360
I had to make an almost funny choice.
"Choose you which you will be—a prude, or puke,
Mewling and puking in the public arms."
"Me for the hills where I don't have to choose."
"But if you had to choose, which would you be?"   365
I wouldn't be a prude afraid of nature.
I know a man who took a double ax
And went alone against a grove of trees;
But his heart failing him, he dropped the ax
And ran for shelter quoting Matthew Arnold: 370
" 'Nature is cruel, man is sick of blood';
There's been enough shed without shedding mine.
Remember Birnam Wood! The wood's in flux!"

170

He had a special terror of the flux
That showed itself in dendrophobia. 375
The only decent tree had been to mill
And educated into boards, he said.
He knew too well for any earthly use
The line where man leaves off and nature starts,
And never overstepped it save in dreams. 380
He stood on the safe side of the line talking—
Which is sheer Matthew Arnoldism,
The cult of one who owned himself "a foiled
Circuitous wanderer," and "took dejectedly
His seat upon the intellectual throne"— 385
Agreed in frowning on these improvised
Altars the woods are full of nowadays,
Again as in the days when Ahaz sinned
By worship under green trees in the open.
Scarcely a mile but that I come on one, 390
A black-cheeked stone and stick of rain-washed charcoal.
Even to say the groves were God's first temples
Comes too near to Ahaz' sin for safety.
Nothing not built with hands of course is sacred.
But here is not a question of what's sacred; 395
Rather of what to face or run away from.
I'd hate to be a runaway from nature.
And neither would I choose to be a puke
Who cares not what he does in company,
And when he can't do anything, falls back 400
On words, and tries his worst to make words speak
Louder than actions, and sometimes achieves it.
It seems a narrow choice the age insists on.
How about being a good Greek, for instance?
That course, they tell me, isn't offered this year. 405
"Come, but this isn't choosing—puke or prude?"

171

Well, if I have to choose one or the other,
I choose to be a plain New Hampshire farmer
With an income in cash of, say, a thousand
(From, say, a publisher in New York City).   410
It's restful to arrive at a decision,
And restful just to think about New Hampshire.
At present I am living in Vermont.

A STAR IN A STONEBOAT

For Lincoln MacVeagh

Never tell me that not one star of all
That slip from heaven at night and softly fall
Has been picked up with stones to build a wall.

Some laborer found one faded and stone-cold,
And saving that its weight suggested gold   5
And tugged it from his first too certain hold,

He noticed nothing in it to remark.
He was not used to handling stars thrown dark
And lifeless from an interrupted arc.

He did not recognize in that smooth coal   10
The one thing palpable besides the soul
To penetrate the air in which we roll.

He did not see how like a flying thing
It brooded ant eggs, and had one large wing,
One not so large for flying in a ring,   15

And a long Bird of Paradise's tail
(Though these when not in use to fly and trail
It drew back in its body like a snail);

172

Nor know that he might move it from the spot—
The harm was done: from having been star-shot   20
The very nature of the soil was hot

And burning to yield flowers instead of grain,
Flowers fanned and not put out by all the rain
Poured on them by his prayers prayed in vain.

He moved it roughly with an iron bar,   25
He loaded an old stoneboat with the star
And not, as you might think, a flying car,

Such as even poets would admit perforce
More practical than Pegasus the horse
If it could put a star back in its course.   30

He dragged it through the plowed ground at a pace
But faintly reminiscent of the race
Of jostling rock in interstellar space.

It went for building stone, and I, as though
Commanded in a dream, forever go   35
To right the wrong that this should have been so.

Yet ask where else it could have gone as well,
I do not know—I cannot stop to tell:
He might have left it lying where it fell.

From following walls I never lift·my eye,   40
Except at night to places in the sky
Where showers of charted meteors let fly.

Some may know what they seek in school and church,
And why they seek it there; for what I search
I must go measuring stone walls, perch on perch; 45

173

Sure that though not a star of death and birth,
So not to be compared, perhaps, in worth
To such resorts of life as Mars and Earth—

Though not, I say, a star of death and sin,
It yet has poles, and only needs a spin   50
To show its worldly nature and begin

To chafe and shuffle in my calloused palm
And run off in strange tangents with my arm,
As fish do with the line in first alarm.

Such as it is, it promises the prize   55
Of the one world complete in any size
That I am like to compass, fool or wise.

THE CENSUS-TAKER

I came an errand one cloud-blowing evening
To a slab-built, black-paper-covered house
Of one room and one window and one door,
The only dwelling in a waste cut over
A hundred square miles round it in the mountains: 5
And that not dwelt in now by men or women.
(It never had been dwelt in, though, by women,
So what is this I make a sorrow of?)
I came as census-taker to the waste
To count the people in it and found none,   10
None in the hundred miles, none in the house,
Where I came last with some hope, but not much,
After hours' overlooking from the cliffs
An emptiness flayed to the very stone.
I found no people that dared show themselves,   15
None not in hiding from the outward eye.

The time was autumn, but how anyone
Could tell the time of year when every tree
That could have dropped a leaf was down itself
And nothing but the stump of it was left   20
Now bringing out its rings in sugar of pitch;
And every tree up stood a rotting trunk
Without a single leaf to spend on autumn,
Or branch to whistle after what was spent.
Perhaps the wind the more without the help   25
Of breathing trees said something of the time
Of year or day the way it swung a door
Forever off the latch, as if rude men
Passed in and slammed it shut each one behind him
For the next one to open for himself.   30
I counted nine I had no right to count
(But this was dreamy unofficial counting)
Before I made the tenth across the threshold.
Where was my supper? Where was anyone's?
No lamp was lit. Nothing was on the table.   35
The stove was cold—the stove was off the chimney—
And down by one side where it lacked a leg.
The people that had loudly passed the door
Were people to the ear but not the eye.
They were not on the table with their elbows.   40
They were not sleeping in the shelves of bunks.
I saw no men there and no bones of men there.
I armed myself against such bones as might be
With the pitch-blackened stub of an ax-handle
I picked up off the straw-dust-covered floor.   45
Not bones, but the ill-fitted window rattled.
The door was still because I held it shut
While I thought what to do that could be done—
About the house—about the people not there.

175

This house in one year fallen to decay 50
Filled me with no less sorrow than the houses
Fallen to ruin in ten thousand years
Where Asia wedges Africa from Europe.
Nothing was left to do that I could see
Unless to find that there was no one there 55
And declare to the cliffs too far for echo,
"The place is desert, and let whoso lurks
In silence, if in this he is aggrieved,
Break silence now or be forever silent.
Let him say why it should not be declared so." 60
The melancholy of having to count souls
Where they grow fewer and fewer every year
Is extreme where they shrink to none at all.
It must be I want life to go on living.

THE STAR-SPLITTER

"You know Orion always comes up sideways.
Throwing a leg up over our fence of mountains,
And rising on his hands, he looks in on me
Busy outdoors by lantern-light with something
I should have done by daylight, and indeed, 5
After the ground is frozen, I should have done
Before it froze, and a gust flings a handful
Of waste leaves at my smoky lantern chimney
To make fun of my way of doing things,
Or else fun of Orion's having caught me. 10
Has a man, I should like to ask, no rights
These forces are obliged to pay respect to?"
So Brad McLaughlin mingled reckless talk
Of heavenly stars with hugger-mugger farming,

176

Till having failed at hugger-mugger farming 15
He burned his house down for the fire insurance
And spent the proceeds on a telescope
To satisfy a lifelong curiosity
About our place among the infinities.

"What do you want with one of those blame things?" 20
I asked him well beforehand. "Don't you get one!"

"Don't call it blamed; there isn't anything
More blameless in the sense of being less
A weapon in our human fight," he said.
"I'll have one if I sell my farm to buy it." 25
There where he moved the rocks to plow the ground
And plowed between the rocks he couldn't move,
Few farms changed hands; so rather than spend years
Trying to sell his farm and then not selling,
He burned his house down for the fire insurance 30
And bought the telescope with what it came to.
He had been heard to say by several:
"The best thing that we're put here for's to see;
The strongest thing that's given us to see with's
A telescope. Someone in every town 35
Seems to me owes it to the town to keep one.
In Littleton it may as well be me."
After such loose talk it was no surprise
When he did what he did and burned his house down.

Mean laughter went about the town that day 40
To let him know we weren't the least imposed on,
And he could wait—we'd see to him tomorrow.
But the first thing next morning we reflected
If one by one we counted people out
For the least sin, it wouldn't take us long 45

177

To get so we had no one left to live with.
For to be social is to be forgiving.
Our thief, the one who does our stealing from us,
We don't cut off from coming to church suppers,
But what we miss we go to him and ask for.   50
He promptly gives it back, that is if still
Uneaten, unworn out, or undisposed of.
It wouldn't do to be too hard on Brad
About his telescope. Beyond the age
Of being given one for Christmas gift,   55
He had to take the best way he knew how
To find himself in one. Well, all we said was
He took a strange thing to be roguish over.
Some sympathy was wasted on the house,
A good old-timer dating back along;   60
But a house isn't sentient; the house
Didn't feel anything. And if it did,
Why not regard it as a sacrifice,
And an old-fashioned sacrifice by fire,
Instead of a new-fashioned one at auction?   65

Out of a house and so out of a farm
At one stroke (of a match), Brad had to turn
To earn a living on the Concord railroad,
As under-ticket-agent at a station
Where his job, when he wasn't selling tickets,   70
Was setting out, up track and down, not plants
As on a farm, but planets, evening stars
That varied in their hue from red to green.

He got a good glass for six hundred dollars.
His new job gave him leisure for stargazing.   75
Often he bid me come and have a look

Up the brass barrel, velvet black inside,
At a star quaking in the other end.
I recollect a night of broken clouds
And underfoot snow melted down to ice,   80
And melting further in the wind to mud.
Bradford and I had out the telescope.
We spread our two legs as we spread its three,
Pointed our thoughts the way we pointed it,
And standing at our leisure till the day broke,   85
Said some of the best things we ever said.
That telescope was christened the Star-Splitter,
Because it didn't do a thing but split
A star in two or three, the way you split
A globule of quicksilver in your hand   90
With one stroke of your finger in the middle.
It's a star-splitter if there ever was one,
And ought to do some good if splitting stars
'Sa thing to be compared with splitting wood.

We've looked and looked, but after all where are we?   95
Do we know any better where we are,
And how it stands between the night tonight
And a man with a smoky lantern chimney?
How different from the way it ever stood?

MAPLE

Her teacher's certainty it must be Mabel
Made Maple first take notice of her name.
She asked her father and he told her, "Maple—
Maple is right."

                    "But teacher told the school
There's no such name."

                    "Teachers don't know as much   5
As fathers about children, you tell teacher.
You tell her that it's M–A–P–L–E.
You ask her if she knows a maple tree.
Well, you were named after a maple tree.
Your mother named you. You and she just saw   10
Each other in passing in the room upstairs,
One coming this way into life, and one
Going the other out of life—you know?
So you can't have much recollection of her.
She had been having a long look at you.   15
She put her finger in your cheek so hard
It must have made your dimple there, and said,
'Maple.' I said it too: 'Yes, for her name.'
She nodded. So we're sure there's no mistake.
I don't know what she wanted it to mean,   20
But it seems like some word she left to bid you
Be a good girl—be like a maple tree.
How like a maple tree's for us to guess.
Or for a little girl to guess sometime.
Not now—at least I shouldn't try too hard now.   25
By and by I will tell you all I know
About the different trees, and something, too,
About your mother that perhaps may help."
Dangerous self-arousing words to sow.
Luckily all she wanted of her name then   30
Was to rebuke her teacher with it next day,
And give the teacher a scare as from her father.
Anything further had been wasted on her,
Or so he tried to think to avoid blame.
She would forget it. She all but forgot it.   35
What he sowed with her slept so long a sleep,
And came so near death in the dark of years,

180

That when it woke and came to life again
The flower was different from the parent seed.
It came back vaguely at the glass one day,   40
As she stood saying her name over aloud,
Striking it gently across her lowered eyes
To make it go well with the way she looked.
What was it about her name? Its strangeness lay
In having too much meaning. Other names,   45
As Lesley, Carol, Irma, Marjorie,
Signified nothing. Rose could have a meaning,
But hadn't as it went. (She knew a Rose.)
This difference from other names it was
Made people notice it—and notice her.   50
(They either noticed it, or got it wrong.)
Her problem was to find out what it asked
In dress or manner of the girl who bore it.
If she could form some notion of her mother—
What she had thought was lovely, and what good.   55
This was her mother's childhood home;
The house one story high in front, three stories
On the end it presented to the road.
(The arrangement made a pleasant sunny cellar.)
Her mother's bedroom was her father's still,   60
Where she could watch her mother's picture fading.
Once she found for a bookmark in the Bible
A maple leaf she thought must have been laid
In wait for her there. She read every word
Of the two pages it was pressed between,   65
As if it was her mother speaking to her.
But forgot to put the leaf back in closing
And lost the place never to read again.
She was sure, though, there had been nothing in it.

181

So she looked for herself, as everyone   70
Looks for himself, more or less outwardly.
And her self-seeking, fitful though it was,
May still have been what led her on to read,
And think a little, and get some city schooling.
She learned shorthand, whatever shorthand may   75
Have had to do with it—she sometimes wondered.
So, till she found herself in a strange place
For the name Maple to have brought her to,
Taking dictation on a paper pad
And, in the pauses when she raised her eyes,   80
Watching out of a nineteenth story window
An airship laboring with unshiplike motion
And a vague all-disturbing roar above the river
Beyond the highest city built with hands.
Someone was saying in such natural tones   85
She almost wrote the words down on her knee,
"Do you know you remind me of a tree—
A maple tree?"

                    "Because my name is Maple?"

"Isn't it Mabel? I thought it was Mabel."

"No doubt you've heard the office call me Mabel.   90
I have to let them call me what they like."

They were both stirred that he should have divined
Without the name her personal mystery.
It made it seem as if there must be something
She must have missed herself. So they were married,   95
And took the fancy home with them to live by.

They went on pilgrimage once to her father's
(The house one story high in front, three stories
On the side it presented to the road)

182

To see if there was not some special tree   100
She might have overlooked. They could find none,
Not so much as a single tree for shade,
Let alone grove of trees for sugar orchard.
She told him of the bookmark maple leaf
In the big Bible, and all she remembered   105
Of the place marked with it—"Wave offering,
Something about wave offering, it said."

"You've never asked your father outright, have you?"

"I have, and been put off sometime, I think."
(This was her faded memory of the way   110
Once long ago her father had put himself off.)

"Because no telling but it may have been
Something between your father and your mother
Not meant for us at all."

          "Not meant for me?
Where would the fairness be in giving me   115
A name to carry for life and never know
The secret of?"

          "And then it may have been
Something a father couldn't tell a daughter
As well as could a mother. And again
It may have been their one lapse into fancy   120
'Twould be too bad to make him sorry for
By bringing it up to him when he was too old.
Your father feels us round him with our questing,
And holds us off unnecessarily,
As if he didn't know what little thing   125
Might lead us on to a discovery.
It was as personal as he could be
About the way he saw it was with you

183

To say your mother, had she lived, would be
As far again as from being born to bearing."   130

"Just one look more with what you say in mind,
And I give up"; which last look came to nothing.
But though they now gave up the search forever,
They clung to what one had seen in the other
By inspiration. It proved there was something.   135
They kept their thoughts away from when the maples
Stood uniform in buckets, and the steam
Of sap and snow rolled off the sugarhouse.
When they made her related to the maples,
It was the tree the autumn fire ran through   140
And swept of leathern leaves, but left the bark
Unscorched, unblackened, even, by any smoke.
They always took their holidays in autumn.
Once they came on a maple in a glade,
Standing alone with smooth arms lifted up,   145
And every leaf of foliage she'd worn
Laid scarlet and pale pink about her feet.
But its age kept them from considering this one.
Twenty-five years ago at Maple's naming
It hardly could have been a two-leaved seedling   150
The next cow might have licked up out at pasture.
Could it have been another maple like it?
They hovered for a moment near discovery,
Figurative enough to see the symbol,
But lacking faith in anything to mean   155
The same at different times to different people.
Perhaps a filial diffidence partly kept them
From thinking it could be a thing so bridal.
And anyway it came too late for Maple.
She used her hands to cover up her eyes.   160

184

"We would not see the secret if we could now:
We are not looking for it any more."

Thus had a name with meaning, given in death,
Made a girl's marriage, and ruled in her life.
No matter that the meaning was not clear.   165
A name with meaning could bring up a child,
Taking the child out of the parents' hands.
Better a meaningless name, I should say,
As leaving more to nature and happy chance.
Name children some names and see what you do.   170

THE AX-HELVE

I've known ere now an interfering branch
Of alder catch my lifted ax behind me.
But that was in the woods, to hold my hand
From striking at another alder's roots,
And that was, as I say, an alder branch.   5
This was a man, Baptiste, who stole one day
Behind me on the snow in my own yard
Where I was working at the chopping block,
And cutting nothing not cut down already.
He caught my ax expertly on the rise,   10
When all my strength put forth was in his favor,
Held it a moment where it was, to calm me,
Then took it from me—and I let him take it.
I didn't know him well enough to know
What it was all about. There might be something   15
He had in mind to say to a bad neighbor
He might prefer to say to him disarmed.
But all he had to tell me in French-English
Was what he thought of—not me, but my ax,

185

Me only as I took my ax to heart.   20
It was the bad ax-helve someone had sold me—
"Made on machine," he said, plowing the grain
With a thick thumbnail to show how it ran
Across the handle's long-drawn serpentine,
Like the two strokes across a dollar sign.   25
"You give her one good crack, she's snap raght off.
Den where's your hax-ead flying t'rough de hair?"
Admitted; and yet, what was that to him?

"Come on my house and I put you one in
What's las' awhile—good hick'ry what's grow crooked,   30
De second growt' I cut myself—tough, tough!"

Something to sell? That wasn't how it sounded.

"Den when you say you come? It's cost you nothing.
Tonaght?"
                As well tonight as any night.

Beyond an over-warmth of kitchen stove   35
My welcome differed from no other welcome.
Baptiste knew best why I was where I was.
So long as he would leave enough unsaid,
I shouldn't mind his being overjoyed
(If overjoyed he was) at having got me   40
Where I must judge if what he knew about an ax
That not everybody else knew was to count
For nothing in the measure of a neighbor.
Hard if, though cast away for life with Yankees,
A Frenchman couldn't get his human rating!   45

Mrs. Baptiste came in and rocked a chair
That had as many motions as the world:
One back and forward, in and out of shadow,

That got her nowhere; one more gradual,
Sideways, that would have run her on the stove   50
In time, had she not realized her danger
And caught herself up bodily, chair and all,
And set herself back where she started from.
"She ain't spick too much Henglish—dat's too bad."
I was afraid, in brightening first on me,   55
Then on Baptiste, as if she understood
What passed between us, she was only feigning.
Baptiste was anxious for her; but no more
Than for himself, so placed he couldn't hope
To keep his bargain of the morning with me   60
In time to keep me from suspecting him
Of really never having meant to keep it.

Needlessly soon he had his ax-helves out,
A quiverful to choose from, since he wished me
To have the best he had, or had to spare—   65
Not for me to ask which, when what he took
Had beauties he had to point me out at length
To insure their not being wasted on me.
He liked to have it slender as a whipstock,
Free from the least knot, equal to the strain   70
Of bending like a sword across the knee.
He showed me that the lines of a good helve
Were native to the grain before the knife
Expressed them, and its curves were no false curves
Put on it from without. And there its strength lay   75
For the hard work. He chafed its long white body
From end to end with his rough hand shut round it.
He tried it at the eyehole in the ax-head.
"Hahn, hahn," he mused, "don't need much taking down."
Baptiste knew how to make a short job long   80

For love of it, and yet not waste time either.

Do you know, what we talked about was knowledge?
Baptiste on his defense about the children
He kept from school, or did his best to keep—
Whatever school and children and our doubts   85
Of laid-on education had to do
With the curves of his ax-helves and his having
Used these unscrupulously to bring me
To see for once the inside of his house.
Was I desired in friendship, partly as someone   90
To leave it to, whether the right to hold
Such doubts of education should depend
Upon the education of those who held them?

But now he brushed the shavings from his knee
And stood the ax there on its horse's hoof,   95
Erect, but not without its waves, as when
The snake stood up for evil in the Garden—
Top-heavy with a heaviness his short,
Thick hand made light of, steel-blue chin drawn down
And in a little—a French touch in that.   100
Baptiste drew back and squinted at it, pleased:
"See how she's cock her head!"

THE GRINDSTONE

Having a wheel and four legs of its own
Has never availed the cumbersome grindstone
To get it anywhere that I can see.
These hands have helped it go, and even race;
Not all the motion, though, they ever lent,   5
Not all the miles it may have thought it went,

188

Have got it one step from the starting place.
It stands beside the same old apple tree.
The shadow of the apple tree is thin
Upon it now; its feet are fast in snow.   10
All other farm machinery's gone in,
And some of it on no more legs and wheel
Than the grindstone can boast to stand or go.
(I'm thinking chiefly of the wheelbarrow.)
For months it hasn't known the taste of steel   15
Washed down with rusty water in a tin.
But standing outdoors hungry, in the cold,
Except in towns at night, is not a sin.
And, anyway, its standing in the yard
Under a ruinous live apple tree   20
Has nothing any more to do with me,
Except that I remember how of old
One summer day, all day I drove it hard,
And someone mounted on it rode it hard,
And he and I between us ground a blade.   25

I gave it the preliminary spin,
And poured on water (tears it might have been);
And when it almost gaily jumped and flowed,
A Father-Time-like man got on and rode,
Armed with a scythe and spectacles that glowed.   30
He turned on willpower to increase the load
And slow me down—and I abruptly slowed,
Like coming to a sudden railroad station.
I changed from hand to hand in desperation.
I wondered what machine of ages gone   35
This represented an improvement on.
For all I knew it may have sharpened spears
And arrowheads itself. Much use for years

189

Had gradually worn it an oblate
Spheroid that kicked and struggled in its gait,   40
Appearing to return me hate for hate
(But I forgive it now as easily
As any other boyhood enemy
Whose pride has failed to get him anywhere).
I wondered who it was the man thought ground—   45
The one who held the wheel back or the one
Who gave his life to keep it going round?
I wondered if he really thought it fair
For him to have the say when we were done.
Such were the bitter thoughts to which I turned.   50

Not for myself was I so much concerned.
Oh no!—although, of course, I could have found
A better way to pass the afternoon
Than grinding discord out of a grindstone,
And beating insects at their gritty tune.   55
Nor was I for the man so much concerned.
Once when the grindstone almost jumped its bearing
It looked as if he might be badly thrown
And wounded on his blade. So far from caring,
I laughed inside, and only cranked the faster   60
(It ran as if it wasn't greased but glued);
I'd welcome any moderate disaster
That might be calculated to postpone
What evidently nothing could conclude.
The thing that made me more and more afraid   65
Was that we'd ground it sharp and hadn't known,
And now were only wasting precious blade.
And when he raised it dripping once and tried
The creepy edge of it with wary touch,
And viewed it over his glasses funny-eyed,   70

190

Only disinterestedly to decide
It needed a turn more, I could have cried
Wasn't there danger of a turn too much?
Mightn't we make it worse instead of better?
I was for leaving something to the whetter.   75
What if it wasn't all it should be? I'd
Be satisfied if he'd be satisfied.

PAUL'S WIFE

To drive Paul out of any lumber camp
All that was needed was to say to him,
"How is the wife, Paul?"—and he'd disappear.
Some said it was because he had no wife,
And hated to be twitted on the subject;   5
Others because he'd come within a day
Or so of having one, and then been jilted;
Others because he'd had one once, a good one,
Who'd run away with someone else and left him;
And others still because he had one now   10
He only had to be reminded of—
He was all duty to her in a minute:
He had to run right off to look her up,
As if to say, "That's so, how is my wife?
I hope she isn't getting into mischief."   15
No one was anxious to get rid of Paul.
He'd been the hero of the mountain camps
Ever since, just to show them, he had slipped
The bark of a whole tamarack off whole,
As clean as boys do off a willow twig   20
To make a willow whistle on a Sunday
In April by subsiding meadow brooks.
They seemed to ask him just to see him go,

"How is the wife, Paul?" and he always went.
He never stopped to murder anyone   25
Who asked the question. He just disappeared—
Nobody knew in what direction,
Although it wasn't usually long
Before they heard of him in some new camp,
The same Paul at the same old feats of logging.   30
The question everywhere was why should Paul
Object to being asked a civil question—
A man you could say almost anything to
Short of a fighting word. You have the answers.
And there was one more not so fair to Paul: 35
That Paul had married a wife not his equal.
Paul was ashamed of her. To match a hero
She would have had to be a heroine;
Instead of which she was some half-breed squaw.
But if the story Murphy told was true,   40
She wasn't anything to be ashamed of.

You know Paul could do wonders. Everyone's
Heard how he thrashed the horses on a load
That wouldn't budge, until they simply stretched
Their rawhide harness from the load to camp.   45
Paul told the boss the load would be all right,
"The sun will bring your load in"—and it did—
By shrinking the rawhide to natural length.
That's what is called a stretcher. But I guess
The one about his jumping so's to land   50
With both his feet at once against the ceiling,
And then land safely right side up again,
Back on the floor, is fact or pretty near fact.
Well, this is such a yarn. Paul sawed his wife
Out of a white-pine log. Murphy was there   55

192

And, as you might say, saw the lady born.
Paul worked at anything in lumbering.
He'd been hard at it taking boards away
For—I forget—the last ambitious sawyer
To want to find out if he couldn't pile   60
The lumber on Paul till Paul begged for mercy.
They'd sliced the first slab off a big butt log,
And the sawyer had slammed the carriage back
To slam end-on again against the saw teeth.
To judge them by the way they caught themselves   65
When they saw what had happened to the log,
They must have had a guilty expectation
Something was going to go with their slambanging.
Something had left a broad black streak of grease
On the new wood the whole length of the log   70
Except, perhaps, a foot at either end.
But when Paul put his finger in the grease,
It wasn't grease at all, but a long slot.
The log was hollow. They were sawing pine.
"First time I ever saw a hollow pine.   75
That comes of having Paul around the place.
Take it to hell for me," the sawyer said.
Everyone had to have a look at it,
And tell Paul what he ought to do about it.
(They treated it as his.) "You take a jackknife,   80
And spread the opening, and you've got a dugout
All dug to go a-fishing in." To Paul
The hollow looked too sound and clean and empty
Ever to have housed birds or beasts or bees.
There was no entrance for them to get in by.   85
It looked to him like some new kind of hollow
He thought he'd *better* take his jackknife to.

So after work that evening he came back
And let enough light into it by cutting
To see if it was empty. He made out in there   90
A slender length of pith, or was it pith?
It might have been the skin a snake had cast
And left stood up on end inside the tree
The hundred years the tree must have been growing.
More cutting and he had this in both hands,   95
And looking from it to the pond nearby,
Paul wondered how it would respond to water.
Not a breeze stirred, but just the breath of air
He made in walking slowly to the beach
Blew it once off his hands and almost broke it.   100
He laid it at the edge, where it could drink.
At the first drink it rustled and grew limp.
At the next drink it grew invisible.
Paul dragged the shallows for it with his fingers,
And thought it must have melted. It was gone.   105
And then beyond the open water, dim with midges,
Where the log drive lay pressed against the boom,
It slowly rose a person, rose a girl,
Her wet hair heavy on her like a helmet,
Who, leaning on a log, looked back at Paul.   110
And that made Paul in turn look back
To see if it was anyone behind him
That she was looking at instead of him.
(Murphy had been there watching all the time,
But from a shed where neither of them could see him.) 115
There was a moment of suspense in birth
When the girl seemed too waterlogged to live,
Before she caught her first breath with a gasp
And laughed. Then she climbed slowly to her feet,

194

And walked off, talking to herself or Paul,   120
Across the logs like backs of alligators,
Paul taking after her around the pond.

Next evening Murphy and some other fellows
Got drunk, and tracked the pair up Catamount,
From the bare top of which there is a view   125
To other hills across a kettle valley.
And there, well after dark, let Murphy tell it,
They saw Paul and his creature keeping house.
It was the only glimpse that anyone
Has had of Paul and her since Murphy saw them   130
Falling in love across the twilight millpond.
More than a mile across the wilderness
They sat together halfway up a cliff
In a small niche let into it, the girl
Brightly, as if a star played on the place,   135
Paul darkly, like her shadow. All the light
Was from the girl herself, though, not from a star,
As was apparent from what happened next.
All those great ruffians put their throats together,
And let out a loud yell, and threw a bottle,   140
As a brute tribute of respect to beauty.
Of course the bottle fell short by a mile,
But the shout reached the girl and put her light out.
She went out like a firefly, and that was all.

So there were witnesses that Paul was married,   145
And not to anyone to be ashamed of.
Everyone had been wrong in judging Paul.
Murphy told me Paul put on all those airs
About his wife to keep her to himself.
Paul was what's called a terrible possessor.   150

195

Owning a wife with him meant owning her.
She wasn't anybody else's business,
Either to praise her or so much as name her,
And he'd thank people not to think of her.
Murphy's idea was that a man like Paul   155
Wouldn't be spoken to about a wife
In any way the world knew how to speak.

WILD GRAPES

What tree may not the fig be gathered from?
The grape may not be gathered from the birch?
It's all you know the grape, or know the birch.
As a girl gathered from the birch myself
Equally with my weight in grapes, one autumn,   5
I ought to know what tree the grape is fruit of.
I was born, I suppose, like anyone,
And grew to be a little boyish girl
My brother could not always leave at home.
But that beginning was wiped out in fear   10
The day I swung suspended with the grapes,
And was come after like Eurydice
And brought down safely from the upper regions;
And the life I live now's an extra life
I can waste as I please on whom I please.   15
So if you see me celebrate two birthdays,
And give myself out as two different ages,
One of them five years younger than I look—

One day my brother led me to a glade
Where a white birch he knew of stood alone,   20
Wearing a thin headdress of pointed leaves,
And heavy on her heavy hair behind,

196

Against her neck, an ornament of grapes.
Grapes, I knew grapes from having seen them last year.
One bunch of them, and there began to be   25
Bunches all round me growing in white birches,
The way they grew round Leif the Lucky's German;
Mostly as much beyond my lifted hands, though,
As the moon used to seem when I was younger,
And only freely to be had for climbing.   30
My brother did the climbing; and at first
Threw me down grapes to miss and scatter
And have to hunt for in sweet fern and hardhack;
Which gave him some time to himself to eat,
But not so much, perhaps, as a boy needed.   35
So then, to make me wholly self-supporting,
He climbed still higher and bent the tree to earth
And put it in my hands to pick my own grapes.
"Here, take a treetop, I'll get down another.
Hold on with all your might when I let go."   40
I said I had the tree. It wasn't true.
The opposite was true. The tree had me.
The minute it was left with me alone,
It caught me up as if I were the fish
And it the fishpole. So I was translated,   45
To loud cries from my brother of "Let go!
Don't you know anything, you girl? Let go!"
But I, with something of the baby grip
Acquired ancestrally in just such trees
When wilder mothers than our wildest now   50
Hung babies out on branches by the hands
To dry or wash or tan, I don't know which
(You'll have to ask an evolutionist)—
I held on uncomplainingly for life.
My brother tried to make me laugh to help me.   55

197

"What are you doing up there in those grapes?
Don't be afraid. A few of them won't hurt you.
I mean, they won't pick you if you don't them."
Much danger of my picking anything!
By that time I was pretty well reduced   60
To a philosophy of hang-and-let-hang.
"Now you know how it feels," my brother said,
"To be a bunch of fox grapes, as they call them,
That when it thinks it has escaped the fox
By growing where it shouldn't—on a birch,   65
Where a fox wouldn't think to look for it—
And if he looked and found it, couldn't reach it—
Just then come you and I to gather it.
Only you have the advantage of the grapes
In one way: you have one more stem to cling by,   70
And promise more resistance to the picker."

One by one I lost off my hat and shoes,
And still I clung. I let my head fall back,
And shut my eyes against the sun, my ears
Against my brother's nonsense. "Drop," he said,   75
"I'll catch you in my arms. It isn't far."
(Stated in lengths of him it might not be.)
"Drop or I'll shake the tree and shake you down."
Grim silence on my part as I sank lower,
My small wrists stretching till they showed the banjo strings.
"Why, if she isn't serious about it!
Hold tight awhile till I think what to do.
I'll bend the tree down and let you down by it."
I don't know much about the letting down;
But once I felt ground with my stocking feet   85
And the world came revolving back to me,
I know I looked long at my curled-up fingers,

198

Before I straightened them and brushed the bark off.
My brother said: "Don't you weigh anything?
Try to weigh something next time, so you won't   90
Be run off with by birch trees into space."

It wasn't my not weighing anything
So much as my not knowing anything—
My brother had been nearer right before.
I had not taken the first step in knowledge;   95
I had not learned to let go with the hands,
As still I have not learned to with the heart,
And have no wish to with the heart—nor need,
That I can see. The mind—is not the heart.
I may yet live, as I know others live,   100
To wish in vain to let go with the mind—
Of cares, at night, to sleep; but nothing tells me
That I need learn to let go with the heart.

PLACE FOR A THIRD

Nothing to say to all those marriages!
She had made three herself to three of his.
The score was even for them, three to three.
But come to die she found she cared so much:
She thought of children in a burial row;   5
Three children in a burial row were sad.
One man's three women in a burial row
Somehow made her impatient with the man.
And so she said to Laban, "You have done
A good deal right; don't do the last thing wrong.   10
Don't make me lie with those two other women."

Laban said, No, he would not make her lie

199

With anyone but that she had a mind to,
If that was how she felt, of course, he said.
She went her way. But Laban having caught   15
This glimpse of lingering person in Eliza,
And anxious to make all he could of it
With something he remembered in himself,
Tried to think how he could exceed his promise,
And give good measure to the dead, though thankless.   20
If that was how she felt, he kept repeating.
His first thought under pressure was a grave
In a new-boughten grave plot by herself,
Under he didn't care how great a stone:
He'd sell a yoke of steers to pay for it.   25
And weren't there special cemetery flowers,
That, once grief sets to growing, grief may rest:
The flowers will go on with grief awhile,
And no one seem neglecting or neglected?
A prudent grief will not despise such aids.   30
He thought of evergreen and everlasting.
And then he had a thought worth many of these.
Somewhere must be the grave of the young boy
Who married her for playmate more than helpmate,
And sometimes laughed at what it was between them.   35
How would she like to sleep her last with him?
Where was his grave? Did Laban know his name?

He found the grave a town or two away,
The headstone cut with *John, Beloved Husband,*
Beside it room reserved; the say a sister's,   40
A never-married sister's of that husband,
Whether Eliza would be welcome there.
The dead was bound to silence: ask the sister.
So Laban saw the sister, and, saying nothing

Of where Eliza wanted *not* to lie,   45
And who had thought to lay her with her first love,
Begged simply for the grave. The sister's face
Fell all in wrinkles of responsibility.
She wanted to do right. She'd have to think.
Laban was old and poor, yet seemed to care;   50
And she was old and poor—but she cared, too.
They sat. She cast one dull, old look at him,
Then turned him out to go on other errands
She said he might attend to in the village,
While she made up her mind how much she cared—   55
And how much Laban cared—and why he cared.
(She made shrewd eyes to see where he came in.)

She'd looked Eliza up her second time,
A widow at her second husband's grave,
And offered her a home to rest awhile   60
Before she went the poor man's widow's way,
Housekeeping for the next man out of wedlock.
She and Eliza had been friends through all.
Who was she to judge marriage in a world
Whose Bible's so confused in marriage counsel?   65
The sister had not come across this Laban;
A decent product of life's ironing-out;
She must not keep him waiting. Time would press
Between the death day and the funeral day.
So when she saw him coming in the street   70
She hurried her decision to be ready
To meet him with his answer at the door.
Laban had known about what it would be
From the way she had set her poor old mouth,
To do, as she had put it, what was right.   75

She gave it through the screen door closed between them:

"No, not with John. There wouldn't be no sense.
Eliza's had too many other men."

Laban was forced to fall back on his plan
To buy Eliza a plot to lie alone in: 80
Which gives him for himself a choice of lots
When his time comes to die and settle down.

TWO WITCHES

I. THE WITCH OF COÖS

I stayed the night for shelter at a farm
Behind the mountain, with a mother and son,
Two old-believers. They did all the talking.

MOTHER.   Folks think a witch who has familiar spirits
She could call up to pass a winter evening,   5
But won't, should be burned at the stake or something.
Summoning spirits isn't "Button, button,
Who's got the button," I would have them know.

SON.   Mother can make a common table rear
And kick with two legs like an army mule.   10

MOTHER.   And when I've done it, what good have I done?
Rather than tip a table for you, let me
Tell you what Ralle the Sioux Control once told me.
He said the dead had souls, but when I asked him
How could that be—I thought the dead were souls—   15
He broke my trance. Don't that make you suspicious
That there's something the dead are keeping back?
Yes, there's something the dead are keeping back.

SON. You wouldn't want to tell him what we have
Up attic, mother?

MOTHER.   Bones—a skeleton.   20

SON. But the headboard of mother's bed is pushed
Against the attic door: the door is nailed.
It's harmless. Mother hears it in the night,
Halting perplexed behind the barrier
Of door and headboard. Where it wants to get   25
Is back into the cellar where it came from.

MOTHER. We'll never let them, will we, son? We'll never!

SON. It left the cellar forty years ago
And carried itself like a pile of dishes
Up one flight from the cellar to the kitchen,   30
Another from the kitchen to the bedroom,
Another from the bedroom to the attic,
Right past both father and mother, and neither stopped it.
Father had gone upstairs; mother was downstairs.
I was a baby: I don't know where I was.   35

MOTHER. The only fault my husband found with me—
I went to sleep before I went to bed,
Especially in winter when the bed
Might just as well be ice and the clothes snow.
The night the bones came up the cellar stairs   40
Toffile had gone to bed alone and left me,
But left an open door to cool the room off
So as to sort of turn me out of it.
I was just coming to myself enough
To wonder where the cold was coming from,   45
When I heard Toffile upstairs in the bedroom
And thought I heard him downstairs in the cellar.

The board we had laid down to walk dry-shod on
When there was water in the cellar in spring
Struck the hard cellar bottom. And then someone   50
Began the stairs, two footsteps for each step,
The way a man with one leg and a crutch,
Or a little child, comes up. It wasn't Toffile:
It wasn't anyone who could be there.
The bulkhead double doors were double-locked   55
And swollen tight and buried under snow.
The cellar windows were banked up with sawdust
And swollen tight and buried under snow.
It was the bones. I knew them—and good reason.
My first impulse was to get to the knob   60
And hold the door. But the bones didn't try
The door; they halted helpless on the landing,
Waiting for things to happen in their favor.
The faintest restless rustling ran all through them.
I never could have done the thing I did   65
If the wish hadn't been too strong in me
To see how they were mounted for this walk.
I had a vision of them put together
Not like a man, but like a chandelier.
So suddenly I flung the door wide on him.   70
A moment he stood balancing with emotion,
And all but lost himself. (A tongue of fire
Flashed out and licked along his upper teeth.
Smoke rolled inside the sockets of his eyes.)
Then he came at me with one hand outstretched,   75
The way he did in life once; but this time
I struck the hand off brittle on the floor,
And fell back from him on the floor myself.
The finger-pieces slid in all directions.

204

(Where did I see one of those pieces lately?   80
Hand me my button box—it must be there.)
I sat up on the floor and shouted, "Toffile,
It's coming up to you." It had its choice
Of the door to the cellar or the hall.
It took the hall door for the novelty,   85
And set off briskly for so slow a thing,
Still going every which way in the joints, though,
So that it looked like lightning or a scribble,
From the slap I had just now given its hand.
I listened till it almost climbed the stairs   90
From the hall to the only finished bedroom,
Before I got up to do anything;
Then ran and shouted, "Shut the bedroom door,
Toffile, for my sake!" "Company?" he said,
"Don't make me get up; I'm too warm in bed."   95
So lying forward weakly on the handrail
I pushed myself upstairs, and in the light
(The kitchen had been dark) I had to own
I could see nothing. "Toffile, I don't see it.
It's with us in the room, though. It's the bones."   100
"What bones?" "The cellar bones—out of the grave."
That made him throw his bare legs out of bed
And sit up by me and take hold of me.
I wanted to put out the light and see
If I could see it, or else mow the room,   105
With our arms at the level of our knees,
And bring the chalk-pile down. "I'll tell you what—
It's looking for another door to try.
The uncommonly deep snow has made him think
Of his old song, 'The Wild Colonial Boy,'   110
He always used to sing along the tote road.
He's after an open door to get outdoors.

205

Let's trap him with an open door up attic."
Toffile agreed to that, and sure enough,
Almost the moment he was given an opening,   115
The steps began to climb the attic stairs.
I heard them. Toffile didn't seem to hear them.
"Quick!" I slammed to the door and held the knob.
"Toffile, get nails." I made him nail the door shut
And push the headboard of the bed against it.   120
Then we asked was there anything
Up attic that we'd ever want again.
The attic was less to us than the cellar.
If the bones liked the attic, let them have it.
Let them stay in the attic. When they sometimes   125
Come down the stairs at night and stand perplexed
Behind the door and headboard of the bed,
Brushing their chalky skull with chalky fingers,
With sounds like the dry rattling of a shutter,
That's what I sit up in the dark to say—   130
To no one anymore since Toffile died.
Let them stay in the attic since they went there.
I promised Toffile to be cruel to them
For helping them be cruel once to him.

SON.   We think they had a grave down in the cellar.   135

MOTHER.   We know they had a grave down in the cellar.

SON.   We never could find out whose bones they were.

MOTHER.   Yes, we could too, son. Tell the truth for once.
They were a man's his father killed for me.
I mean a man he killed instead of me.   140
The least I could do was help dig their grave.
We were about it one night in the cellar.
Son knows the story: but 'twas not for him

To tell the truth, suppose the time had come.
Son looks surprised to see me end a lie 145
We'd kept up all these years between ourselves
So as to have it ready for outsiders.
But tonight I don't care enough to lie—
I don't remember why I ever cared.
Toffile, if he were here, I don't believe 150
Could tell you why he ever cared himself. . . .

She hadn't found the finger-bone she wanted
Among the buttons poured out in her lap.
I verified the name next morning: Toffile.
The rural letter box said Toffile Lajway. 155

II.   THE PAUPER WITCH OF GRAFTON

Now that they've got it settled whose I be,
I'm going to tell them something they won't like:
They've got it settled wrong, and I can prove it.
Flattered I must be to have two towns fighting
To make a present of me to each other. 5
They don't dispose me, either one of them,
To spare them any trouble. Double trouble's
Always the witch's motto anyway.
I'll double theirs for both of them—you watch me.
They'll find they've got the whole thing to do over, 10
That is, if facts is what they want to go by.
They set a lot (now don't they?) by a record
Of Arthur Amy's having once been up
For Hog Reeve in March Meeting here in Warren.
I could have told them any time this twelvemonth 15
The Arthur Amy I was married to
Couldn't have been the one they say was up

207

In Warren at March Meeting, for the reason
He wa'n't but fifteen at the time they say.
The Arthur Amy I was married to   20
Voted the only times he ever voted,
Which wasn't many, in the town of Wentworth.
One of the times was when 'twas in the warrant
To see if the town wanted to take over
The tote road to our clearing where we lived.   25
I'll tell you who'd remember—Heman Lapish.
Their Arthur Amy was the father of mine.
So now they've dragged it through the law courts once,
I guess they'd better drag it through again.
Wentworth and Warren's both good towns to live in,   30
Only I happen to prefer to live
In Wentworth from now on; and when all's said,
Right's right, and the temptation to do right
When I can hurt someone by doing it
Has always been too much for me, it has.   35
I know of some folks that'd be set up
At having in their town a noted witch:
But most would have to think of the expense
That even I would be. They ought to know
That as a witch I'd often milk a bat   40
And that'd be enough to last for days.
It'd make my position stronger, think,
If I was to consent to give some sign
To make it surer that I was a witch?
It wa'n't no sign, I s'pose, when Mallice Huse   45
Said that I took him out in his old age
And rode all over everything on him
Until I'd had him worn to skin and bones,
And if I'd left him hitched unblanketed
In front of one Town Hall, I'd left him hitched   50

208

In front of every one in Grafton County.
Some cried shame on me not to blanket him,
The poor old man. It would have been all right
If someone hadn't said to gnaw the posts
He stood beside and leave his trademark on them,   55
So they could recognize them. Not a post
That they could hear tell of was scarified.
They made him keep on gnawing till he whined.
Then that same smarty someone said to look—
He'd bet Huse was a cribber and had gnawed   60
The crib he slept in—and as sure's you're born
They found he'd gnawed the four posts of his bed,
All four of them to splinters. What did that prove?
Not that he hadn't gnawed the hitching posts
He said he had, besides. Because a horse   65
Gnaws in the stable ain't no proof to me
He don't gnaw trees and posts and fences too.
But everybody took it for a proof.
I was a strapping girl of twenty then.
The smarty someone who spoiled everything   70
Was Arthur Amy. You know who he was.
That was the way he started courting me.
He never said much after we were married,
But I mistrusted he was none too proud
Of having interfered in the Huse business.   75
I guess he found he got more out of me
By having me a witch. Or something happened
To turn him round. He got to saying things
To undo what he'd done and make it right,
Like, "No, she ain't come back from kiting yet.   80
Last night was one of her nights out. She's kiting.
She thinks when the wind makes a night of it
She might as well herself." But he liked best

209

To let on he was plagued to death with me:
If anyone had seen me coming home   85
Over the ridgepole, 'stride of a broomstick,
As often as he had in the tail of the night,
He guessed they'd know what he had to put up with.
Well, I showed Arthur Amy signs enough
Off from the house as far as we could keep   90
And from barn smells you can't wash out of plowed ground
With all the rain and snow of seven years;
And I don't mean just skulls of Rogers' Rangers
On Moosilauke, but woman signs to man,
Only bewitched so I would last him longer.   95
Up where the trees grow short, the mosses tall,
I made him gather me wet snowberries
On slippery rocks beside a waterfall.
I made him do it for me in the dark.
And he liked everything I made him do.   100
I hope if he is where he sees me now
He's so far off he can't see what I've come to.
You *can* come down from everything to nothing.
All is, if I'd a-known when I was young
And full of it, that this would be the end,   105
It doesn't seem as if I'd had the courage
To make so free and kick up in folks' faces.
I might have, but it doesn't seem as if.

AN EMPTY THREAT

I stay;
But it isn't as if
There wasn't always Hudson's Bay
And the fur trade,

210

A small skiff   5
And a paddle blade.

I can just see my tent pegged,
And me on the floor,
Cross-legged,
And a trapper looking in at the door   10
With furs to sell.

His name's Joe,
Alias John,
And between what he doesn't know
And won't tell   15
About where Henry Hudson's gone,
I can't say he's much help;
But we get on.

The seal yelp
On an ice cake.   20
It's not men by some mistake?

No,
There's not a soul
For a windbreak
Between me and the North Pole—   25

Except always John-Joe,
My French Indian Esquimaux,
And he's off setting traps—
In one himself perhaps.

Give a headshake   30
Over so much bay
Thrown away
In snow and mist
That doesn't exist,

211

I was going to say,   35
For God, man, or beast's sake,
Yet does perhaps for all three.

Don't ask Joe
What it is to him.
It's sometimes dim   40
What it is to me,
Unless it be
It's the old captain's dark fate
Who failed to find or force a strait
In its two-thousand-mile coast;   45
And his crew left him where he failed,
And nothing came of all he sailed.

It's to say, "You and I—"
To such a ghost—
"You and I   50
Off here
With the dead race of the Great Auk!"
And, "Better defeat almost,
If seen clear,
Than life's victories of doubt   55
That need endless talk-talk
To make them out."

A FOUNTAIN, A BOTTLE,
A DONKEY'S EARS, AND SOME BOOKS

Old Davis owned a solid mica mountain
In Dalton that would someday make his fortune.
There'd been some Boston people out to see it:
And experts said that deep down in the mountain

212

The mica sheets were big as plate-glass windows.   5
He'd like to take me there and show it to me.

"I'll tell you what you show me. You remember
You said you knew the place where once, on Kinsman,
The early Mormons made a settlement
And built a stone baptismal font outdoors—   10
But Smith, or someone, called them off the mountain
To go West to a worse fight with the desert.
You said you'd seen the stone baptismal font.
Well, take me there."

               "Someday I will."

                    "Today."

"Huh, that old bathtub, what is that to see?   15
Let's talk about it."

            "Let's go see the place."

"To shut you up I'll tell you what I'll do:
I'll find that fountain if it takes all summer,
And both of our united strengths, to do it."

"You've lost it, then?"

              "Not so but I can find it.   20
No doubt it's grown up some to woods around it.
The mountain may have shifted since I saw it
In eighty-five."

         "As long ago as that?"

"If I remember rightly, it had sprung
A leak and emptied then. And forty years   25
Can do a good deal to bad masonry.
You won't see any Mormon swimming in it.
But you have said it, and we're off to find it.

213

Old as I am, I'm going to let myself
Be dragged by you all over everywhere——"

"I thought you were a guide."

                        "I *am* a guide,
And that's why I can't decently refuse you."

We made a day of it out of the world,
Ascending to descend to reascend.
The old man seriously took his bearings,   35
And spoke his doubts in every open place.

We came out on a look-off where we faced
A cliff, and on the cliff a bottle painted,
Or stained by vegetation from above,
A likeness to surprise the thrilly tourist.   40

"Well, if I haven't brought you to the fountain,
At least I've brought you to the famous Bottle."

"I won't accept the substitute. It's empty."

"So's everything."

                "I want my fountain."

"I guess you'd find the fountain just as empty.   45
And anyway this tells me where I am."

"Hadn't you long suspected where you were?"

"You mean miles from that Mormon settlement?
Look here, you treat your guide with due respect
If you don't want to spend the night outdoors.   50
I vow we must be near the place from where
The two converging slides, the avalanches,
On Marshall, look like donkey's ears.
We may as well see that and save the day."

"Don't donkey's ears suggest we shake our own?"   55

"For God's sake, aren't you fond of viewing nature?
You don't like nature. All you like is books.
What signify a donkey's ears and bottle,
However natural? Give you your books!
Well then, right here is where I show you books.   60
Come straight down off this mountain just as fast
As we can fall and keep a-bouncing on our feet.
It's hell for knees unless done hell-for-leather."

Be ready, I thought, for almost anything.

We struck a road I didn't recognize,   65
But welcomed for the chance to lave my shoes
In dust once more. We followed this a mile,
Perhaps, to where it ended at a house
I didn't know was there. It was the kind
To bring me to for broad-board paneling.   70
I never saw so good a house deserted.

"Excuse me if I ask you in a window
That happens to be broken," Davis said.
"The outside doors as yet have held against us.
I want to introduce you to the people   75
Who used to live here. They were Robinsons.
You must have heard of Clara Robinson,
The poetess who wrote the book of verses
And had it published. It was all about
The posies on her inner windowsill,   80
And the birds on her outer windowsill,
And how she tended both, or had them tended:
She never tended anything herself.
She was 'shut in' for life. She lived her whole
Life long in bed, and wrote her things in bed.   85

215

I'll show you how she had her sills extended
To entertain the birds and hold the flowers.
Our business first's up attic with her books."

We trod uncomfortably on crunching glass
Through a house stripped of everything   90
Except, it seemed, the poetess's poems.
Books, I should say!—if books are what is needed.
A whole edition in a packing case
That, overflowing like a horn of plenty,
Or like the poetess's heart of love,   95
Had spilled them near the window, toward the light,
Where driven rain had wet and swollen them.
Enough to stock a village library—
Unfortunately all of one kind, though.
They had been brought home from some publisher   100
And taken thus into the family.
Boys and bad hunters had known what to do
With stone and lead to unprotected glass:
Shatter it inward on the unswept floors.
How had the tender verse escaped their outrage?   105
By being invisible for what it was,
Or else by some remoteness that defied them
To find out what to do to hurt a poem.
Yet oh! the tempting flatness of a book,
To send it sailing out the attic window   110
Till it caught wind and, opening out its covers,
Tried to improve on sailing like a tile
By flying like a bird (silent in flight,
But all the burden of its body song),
Only to tumble like a stricken bird,   115
And lie in stones and bushes unretrieved.
Books were not thrown irreverently about.

216

They simply lay where someone now and then,
Having tried one, had dropped it at his feet
And left it lying where it fell rejected.   120
Here were all those the poetess's life
Had been too short to sell or give away.

"Take one," Old Davis bade me graciously.

"Why not take two or three?"
                              "Take all you want.
Good-looking books like that." He picked one fresh   125
In virgin wrapper from deep in the box,
And stroked it with a horny-handed kindness.
He read in one and I read in another,
Both either looking for or finding something.

The attic wasps went missing by like bullets.   130

I was soon satisfied for the time being.

All the way home I kept remembering
The small book in my pocket. It was there.
The poetess had sighed, I knew, in heaven
At having eased her heart of one more copy—   135
Legitimately. My demand upon her,
Though slight, was a demand. She felt the tug.
In time she would be rid of all her books.

I WILL SING YOU ONE-O

It was long I lay
Awake that night
Wishing the tower
Would name the hour
And tell me whether   5

To call it day
(Though not yet light)
And give up sleep.
The snow fell deep
With the hiss of spray;   10
Two winds would meet,
One down one street,
One down another,
And fight in a smother
Of dust and feather.   15
I could not say,
But feared the cold
Had checked the pace
Of the tower clock
By tying together   20
Its hands of gold
Before its face.

Then came one knock!
A note unruffled
Of earthly weather,   25
Though strange and muffled.
The tower said, "One!"
And then a steeple.
They spoke to themselves
And such few people   30
As winds might rouse
From sleeping warm
(But not unhouse).
They left the storm
That struck en masse   35
My window glass
Like a beaded fur.

218

In that grave One
They spoke of the sun
And moon and stars,   40
Saturn and Mars
And Jupiter.
Still more unfettered,
They left the named
And spoke of the lettered,   45
The sigmas and taus
Of constellations.
They filled their throats
With the furthest bodies
To which man sends his   50
Speculation,
Beyond which God is;
The cosmic motes
Of yawning lenses.
Their solemn peals   55
Were not their own:
They spoke for the clock
With whose vast wheels
Theirs interlock.
In that grave word   60
Uttered alone
The utmost star
Trembled and stirred,
Though set so far
Its whirling frenzies   65
Appear like standing
In one self station.
It has not ranged,
And save for the wonder
Of once expanding   70

219

To be a nova,
It has not changed
To the eye of man
On planets over,
Around, and under   75
It in creation
Since man began
To drag down man
And nation nation.

FRAGMENTARY BLUE

Why make so much of fragmentary blue
In here and there a bird, or butterfly,
Or flower, or wearing-stone, or open eye,
When heaven presents in sheets the solid hue?

Since earth is earth, perhaps, not heaven (as yet)—   5
Though some savants make earth include the sky;
And blue so far above us comes so high,
It only gives our wish for blue a whet.

FIRE AND ICE

Some say the world will end in fire,
Some say in ice.
From what I've tasted of desire
I hold with those who favor fire.
But if it had to perish twice,   5
I think I know enough of hate
To say that for destruction ice
Is also great
And would suffice.

IN A DISUSED GRAVEYARD

The living come with grassy tread
To read the gravestones on the hill;
The graveyard draws the living still,
But never anymore the dead.

The verses in it say and say: 5
"The ones who living come today
To read the stones and go away
Tomorrow dead will come to stay."

So sure of death the marbles rhyme,
Yet can't help marking all the time   10
How no one dead will seem to come.
What is it men are shrinking from?

It would be easy to be clever
And tell the stones: Men hate to die
And have stopped dying now forever.   15
I think they would believe the lie.

DUST OF SNOW

The way a crow
Shook down on me
The dust of snow
From a hemlock tree

Has given my heart   5
A change of mood
And saved some part
Of a day I had rued.

221

TO E.T.

I slumbered with your poems on my breast,
Spread open as I dropped them half-read through
Like dove wings on a figure on a tomb,
To see if in a dream they brought of you

I might not have the chance I missed in life   5
Through some delay, and call you to your face
First soldier, and then poet, and then both,
Who died a soldier-poet of your race.

I meant, you meant, that nothing should remain
Unsaid between us, brother, and this remained—   10
And one thing more that was not then to say:
The Victory for what it lost and gained.

You went to meet the shell's embrace of fire
On Vimy Ridge; and when you fell that day
The war seemed over more for you than me,   15
But now for me than you—the other way.

How over, though, for even me who knew
The foe thrust back unsafe beyond the Rhine,
If I was not to speak of it to you
And see you pleased once more with words of mine?   20

NOTHING GOLD CAN STAY

Nature's first green is gold,
Her hardest hue to hold.
Her early leaf's a flower;
But only so an hour.
Then leaf subsides to leaf.   5
So Eden sank to grief,

222

So dawn goes down to day.
Nothing gold can stay.

THE RUNAWAY

Once when the snow of the year was beginning to fall,
We stopped by a mountain pasture to say, "Whose colt?"
A little Morgan had one forefoot on the wall,
The other curled at his breast. He dipped his head
And snorted at us. And then he had to bolt.   5
We heard the miniature thunder where he fled,
And we saw him, or thought we saw him, dim and gray,
Like a shadow against the curtain of falling flakes.
"I think the little fellow's afraid of the snow.
He isn't winter-broken. It isn't play   10
With the little fellow at all. He's running away.
I doubt if even his mother could tell him, 'Sakes,
It's only weather.' He'd think she didn't know!
Where is his mother? He can't be out alone."
And now he comes again with clatter of stone,   15
And mounts the wall again with whited eyes
And all his tail that isn't hair up straight.
He shudders his coat as if to throw off flies.
"Whoever it is that leaves him out so late,
When other creatures have gone to stall and bin,   20
Ought to be told to come and take him in."

THE AIM WAS SONG

Before man came to blow it right
    The wind once blew itself untaught,
And did its loudest day and night
    In any rough place where it caught.

223

Man came to tell it what was wrong: 5
    It hadn't found the place to blow;
It blew too hard—the aim was song.
    And listen—how it ought to go!

He took a little in his mouth,
    And held it long enough for north   10
To be converted into south,
    And then by measure blew it forth.

By measure. It was word and note,
    The wind the wind had meant to be—
A little through the lips and throat.   15
    The aim was song—the wind could see.

STOPPING BY WOODS
ON A SNOWY EVENING

Whose woods these are I think I know.
His house is in the village, though;
He will not see me stopping here
To watch his woods fill up with snow.

My little horse must think it queer   5
To stop without a farmhouse near
Between the woods and frozen lake
The darkest evening of the year.

He gives his harness bells a shake
To ask if there is some mistake.   10
The only other sound's the sweep
Of easy wind and downy flake.

The woods are lovely, dark, and deep,

But I have promises to keep,
And miles to go before I sleep,   15
And miles to go before I sleep.

FOR ONCE, THEN, SOMETHING

Others taunt me with having knelt at well-curbs
Always wrong to the light, so never seeing
Deeper down in the well than where the water
Gives me back in a shining surface picture
Me myself in the summer heaven, godlike,   5
Looking out of a wreath of fern and cloud puffs.
Once, when trying with chin against a well-curb,
I discerned, as I thought, beyond the picture,
Through the picture, a something white, uncertain,
Something more of the depths—and then I lost it.   10
Water came to rebuke the too clear water.
One drop fell from a fern, and lo, a ripple
Shook whatever it was lay there at bottom,
Blurred it, blotted it out. What was that whiteness?
Truth? A pebble of quartz? For once, then, something. 15

BLUE-BUTTERFLY DAY

It is blue-butterfly day here in spring,
And with these sky-flakes down in flurry on flurry
There is more unmixed color on the wing
Than flowers will show for days unless they hurry.

But these are flowers that fly and all but sing: 5
And now from having ridden out desire
They lie closed over in the wind and cling
Where wheels have freshly sliced the April mire.

225

THE ONSET

Always the same, when on a fated night
At last the gathered snow lets down as white
As may be in dark woods, and with a song
It shall not make again all winter long
Of hissing on the yet uncovered ground,   5
I almost stumble looking up and round,
As one who overtaken by the end
Gives up his errand, and lets death descend
Upon him where he is, with nothing done
To evil, no important triumph won,   10
More than if life had never been begun.

Yet all the precedent is on my side:
I know that winter death has never tried
The earth but it has failed: the snow may heap
In long storms an undrifted four feet deep   15
As measured against maple, birch, and oak,
It cannot check the peeper's silver croak;
And I shall see the snow all go downhill
In water of a slender April rill
That flashes tail through last year's withered brake   20
And dead weeds, like a disappearing snake.
Nothing will be left white but here a birch,
And there a clump of houses with a church.

TO EARTHWARD

Love at the lips was touch
As sweet as I could bear;
And once that seemed too much;
I lived on air

That crossed me from sweet things,   5
The flow of—was it musk
From hidden grapevine springs
Downhill at dusk?

I had the swirl and ache
From sprays of honeysuckle   10
That when they're gathered shake
Dew on the knuckle.

I craved strong sweets, but those
Seemed strong when I was young;
The petal of the rose   15
It was that stung.

Now no joy but lacks salt,
That is not dashed with pain
And weariness and fault;
I crave the stain   20

Of tears, the aftermark
Of almost too much love,
The sweet of bitter bark
And burning clove.

When stiff and sore and scarred   25
I take away my hand
From leaning on it hard
In grass and sand,

The hurt is not enough:
I long for weight and strength   30
To feel the earth as rough
To all my length.

GOOD-BY AND KEEP COLD

This saying good-by on the edge of the dark
And the cold to an orchard so young in the bark
Reminds me of all that can happen to harm
An orchard away at the end of the farm
All winter, cut off by a hill from the house.   5
I don't want it girdled by rabbit and mouse,
I don't want it dreamily nibbled for browse
By deer, and I don't want it budded by grouse.
(If certain it wouldn't be idle to call
I'd summon grouse, rabbit, and deer to the wall   10
And warn them away with a stick for a gun.)
I don't want it stirred by the heat of the sun.
(We made it secure against being, I hope,
By setting it out on a northerly slope.)
No orchard's the worse for the wintriest storm;   15
But one thing about it, it mustn't get warm.
"How often already you've had to be told,
Keep cold, young orchard. Good-by and keep cold.
Dread fifty above more than fifty below."
I have to be gone for a season or so.   20
My business awhile is with different trees,
Less carefully nurtured, less fruitful than these,
And such as is done to their wood with an ax—
Maples and birches and tamaracks.
I wish I could promise to lie in the night   25
And think of an orchard's arboreal plight
When slowly (and nobody comes with a light)
Its heart sinks lower under the sod.
But something has to be left to God.

228

TWO LOOK AT TWO

Love and forgetting might have carried them
A little further up the mountainside
With night so near, but not much further up.
They must have halted soon in any case
With thoughts of the path back, how rough it was   5
With rock and washout, and unsafe in darkness;
When they were halted by a tumbled wall
With barbed-wire binding. They stood facing this,
Spending what onward impulse they still had
In one last look the way they must not go,   10
On up the failing path, where, if a stone
Or earthslide moved at night, it moved itself;
No footstep moved it. "This is all," they sighed,
"Good-night to woods." But not so; there was more.
A doe from round a spruce stood looking at them   15
Across the wall, as near the wall as they.
She saw them in their field, they her in hers.
The difficulty of seeing what stood still,
Like some up-ended boulder split in two,
Was in her clouded eyes: they saw no fear there.   20
She seemed to think that, two thus, they were safe.
Then, as if they were something that, though strange,
She could not trouble her mind with too long,
She sighed and passed unscared along the wall.
"*This*, then, is all. What more is there to ask?"   25
But no, not yet. A snort to bid them wait.
A buck from round the spruce stood looking at them
Across the wall, as near the wall as they.
This was an antlered buck of lusty nostril,
Not the same doe come back into her place.   30
He viewed them quizzically with jerks of head,

229

As if to ask, "Why don't you make some motion?
Or give some sign of life? Because you can't.
I doubt if you're as living as you look."
Thus till he had them almost feeling dared   35
To stretch a proffering hand—and a spell-breaking.
Then he too passed unscared along the wall.
Two had seen two, whichever side you spoke from.
"This *must* be all." It was all. Still they stood,
A great wave from it going over them,   40
As if the earth in one unlooked-for favor
Had made them certain earth returned their love.

NOT TO KEEP

They sent him back to her. The letter came
Saying. . . . And she could have him. And before
She could be sure there was no hidden ill
Under the formal writing, he was there,
Living. They gave him back to her alive—   5
How else? They are not known to send the dead.—
And not disfigured visibly. His face?
His hands? She had to look, to look and ask,
"What is it, dear?" And she had given all
And still she had all—*they* had—they the lucky!   10
Wasn't she glad now? Everything seemed won,
And all the rest for them permissible ease.
She had to ask, "What was it, dear?"

                      "Enough,
Yet not enough. A bullet through and through,
High in the breast. Nothing but what good care   15
And medicine and rest, and you a week,
Can cure me of to go again." The same

230

Grim giving to do over for them both.
She dared no more than ask him with her eyes
How was it with him for a second trial.   20
And with his eyes he asked her not to ask.
They had given him back to her, but not to keep.

A BROOK IN THE CITY

The farmhouse lingers, though averse to square
With the new city street it has to wear
A number in. But what about the brook
That held the house as in an elbow-crook?
I ask as one who knew the brook, its strength   5
And impulse, having dipped a finger length
And made it leap my knuckle, having tossed
A flower to try its currents where they crossed.
The meadow grass could be cemented down
From growing under pavements of a town;   10
The apple trees be sent to hearthstone flame.
Is water wood to serve a brook the same?
How else dispose of an immortal force
No longer needed? Staunch it at its source
With cinder loads dumped down? The brook was thrown
Deep in a sewer dungeon under stone
In fetid darkness still to live and run—
And all for nothing it had ever done,
Except forget to go in fear perhaps.
No one would know except for ancient maps   20
That such a brook ran water. But I wonder
If from its being kept forever under,
The thoughts may not have risen that so keep
This new-built city from both work and sleep.

231

THE KITCHEN CHIMNEY

Builder, in building the little house,
In every way you may please yourself;
But please please me in the kitchen chimney:
Don't build me a chimney upon a shelf.

However far you must go for bricks,   5
Whatever they cost apiece or a pound,
Buy me enough for a full-length chimney,
And build the chimney clear from the ground.

It's not that I'm greatly afraid of fire,
But I never heard of a house that throve   10
(And I know of one that didn't thrive)
Where the chimney started above the stove.

And I dread the ominous stain of tar
That there always is on the papered walls,
And the smell of fire drowned in rain   15
That there always is when the chimney's false.

A shelf's for a clock or vase or picture,
But I don't see why it should have to bear
A chimney that only would serve to remind me
Of castles I used to build in air.   20

LOOKING FOR A SUNSET BIRD
IN WINTER

The west was getting out of gold,
The breath of air had died of cold,
When shoeing home across the white,
I thought I saw a bird alight.

In summer when I passed the place, 5
I had to stop and lift my face;
A bird with an angelic gift
Was singing in it sweet and swift.

No bird was singing in it now.
A single leaf was on a bough, 10
And that was all there was to see
In going twice around the tree.

From my advantage on a hill
I judged that such a crystal chill
Was only adding frost to snow 15
As gilt to gold that wouldn't show.

A brush had left a crooked stroke
Of what was either cloud or smoke
From north to south across the blue;
A piercing little star was through. 20

A BOUNDLESS MOMENT

He halted in the wind, and—what was that
Far in the maples, pale, but not a ghost?
He stood there bringing March against his thought,
And yet too ready to believe the most.

"Oh, that's the Paradise-in-Bloom," I said; 5
And truly it was fair enough for flowers
Had we but in us to assume in March
Such white luxuriance of May for ours.

We stood a moment so, in a strange world,
Myself as one his own pretense deceives; 10

233

And then I said the truth (and we moved on).
A young beech clinging to its last year's leaves.

EVENING IN A SUGAR ORCHARD

From where I lingered in a lull in March
Outside the sugarhouse one night for choice,
I called the fireman with a careful voice
And bade him leave the pan and stoke the arch:
"O fireman, give the fire another stoke,   5
And send more sparks up chimney with the smoke."
I thought a few might tangle, as they did,
Among bare maple boughs, and in the rare
Hill atmosphere not cease to glow,
And so be added to the moon up there.   10
The moon, though slight, was moon enough to show
On every tree a bucket with a lid,
And on black ground a bear-skin rug of snow.
The sparks made no attempt to be the moon.
They were content to figure in the trees   15
As Leo, Orion, and the Pleiades.
And that was what the boughs were full of soon.

GATHERING LEAVES

Spades take up leaves
No better than spoons,
And bags full of leaves
Are light as balloons.

I make a great noise   5
Of rustling all day

234

Like rabbit and deer
Running away.

But the mountains I raise
Elude my embrace,   10
Flowing over my arms
And into my face.

I may load and unload
Again and again
Till I fill the whole shed,   15
And what have I then?

Next to nothing for weight;
And since they grew duller
From contact with earth,
Next to nothing for color.   20

Next to nothing for use.
But a crop is a crop,
And who's to say where
The harvest shall stop?

THE VALLEY'S SINGING DAY

The sound of the closing outside door was all.
You made no sound in the grass with your footfall,
As far as you went from the door, which was not far;
But you had awakened under the morning star
The first songbird that awakened all the rest.   5
He could have slept but a moment more at best.
Already determined dawn began to lay
In place across a cloud the slender ray
For prying beneath and forcing the lids of sight,

235

And loosing the pent-up music of overnight.   10
But dawn was not to begin their "pearly-pearly"
(By which they mean the rain is pearls so early,
Before it changes to diamonds in the sun),
Neither was song that day to be self-begun.
You had begun it, and if there needed proof—   15
I was asleep still under the dripping roof,
My window curtain hung over the sill to wet;
But I should awake to confirm your story yet;
I should be willing to say and help you say
That once you had opened the valley's singing day.   20

MISGIVING

All crying, "We will go with you, O Wind!"
The foliage follow him, leaf and stem;
But a sleep oppresses them as they go,
And they end by bidding him stay with them.

Since ever they flung abroad in spring   5
The leaves had promised themselves this flight,
Who now would fain seek sheltering wall,
Or thicket, or hollow place for the night.

And now they answer his summoning blast
With an ever vaguer and vaguer stir,   10
Or at utmost a little reluctant whirl
That drops them no further than where they were.

I only hope that when I am free,
As they are free, to go in quest
Of the knowledge beyond the bounds of life   15
It may not seem better to me to rest.

236

A HILLSIDE THAW

To think to know the country and not know
The hillside on the day the sun lets go
Ten million silver lizards out of snow!
As often as I've seen it done before
I can't pretend to tell the way it's done. 5
It looks as if some magic of the sun
Lifted the rug that bred them on the floor
And the light breaking on them made them run.
But if I thought to stop the wet stampede,
And caught one silver lizard by the tail, 10
And put my foot on one without avail,
And threw myself wet-elbowed and wet-kneed
In front of twenty others' wriggling speed—
In the confusion of them all aglitter,
And birds that joined in the excited fun 15
By doubling and redoubling song and twitter—
I have no doubt I'd end by holding none.

It takes the moon for this. The sun's a wizard
By all I tell; but so's the moon a witch.
From the high west she makes a gentle cast 20
And suddenly, without a jerk or twitch,
She has her spell on every single lizard.
I fancied when I looked at six o'clock
The swarm still ran and scuttled just as fast.
The moon was waiting for her chill effect. 25
I looked at nine: the swarm was turned to rock
In every lifelike posture of the swarm,
Transfixed on mountain slopes almost erect.
Across each other and side by side they lay.
The spell that so could hold them as they were 30

Was wrought through trees without a breath of storm
To make a leaf, if there had been one, stir.
It was the moon's: she held them until day,
One lizard at the end of every ray.
The thought of my attempting such a stay! 35

PLOWMEN

A plow, they say, to plow the snow.
They cannot mean to plant it, no—
Unless in bitterness to mock
At having cultivated rock.

ON A TREE FALLEN ACROSS THE ROAD

(To hear us talk)

The tree the tempest with a crash of wood
Throws down in front of us is not to bar
Our passage to our journey's end for good,
But just to ask us who we think we are

Insisting always on our own way so. 5
She likes to halt us in our runner tracks,
And make us get down in a foot of snow
Debating what to do without an ax.

And yet she knows obstruction is in vain:
We will not be put off the final goal 10
We have it hidden in us to attain,
Not though we have to seize earth by the pole

And, tired of aimless circling in one place,
Steer straight off after something into space.

238

OUR SINGING STRENGTH

It snowed in spring on earth so dry and warm
The flakes could find no landing place to form.
Hordes spent themselves to make it wet and cold,
And still they failed of any lasting hold.
They made no white impression on the black.   5
They disappeared as if earth sent them back.
Not till from separate flakes they changed at night
To almost strips and tapes of ragged white
Did grass and garden ground confess it snowed,
And all go back to winter but the road.   10
Next day the scene was piled and puffed and dead.
The grass lay flattened under one great tread.
Borne down until the end almost took root,
The rangey bough anticipated fruit
With snowballs cupped in every opening bud.   15
The road alone maintained itself in mud,
Whatever its secret was of greater heat
From inward fires or brush of passing feet.

In spring more mortal singers than belong
To any one place cover us with song.   20
Thrush, bluebird, blackbird, sparrow, and robin throng;
Some to go further north to Hudson's Bay,
Some that have come too far north back away,
Really a very few to build and stay.
Now was seen how these liked belated snow.   25
The fields had nowhere left for them to go;
They'd soon exhausted all there was in flying;
The trees they'd had enough of with once trying
And setting off their heavy powder load.
They could find nothing open but the road.   30

239

So there they let their lives be narrowed in
By thousands the bad weather made akin.
The road became a channel running flocks
Of glossy birds like ripples over rocks.
I drove them underfoot in bits of flight   35
That kept the ground, almost disputing right
Of way with me from apathy of wing,
A talking twitter all they had to sing.
A few I must have driven to despair
Made quick asides, but having done in air   40
A whir among white branches great and small,
As in some too much carven marble hall
Where one false wing beat would have brought down all,
Came tamely back in front of me, the Drover,
To suffer the same driven nightmare over.   45
One such storm in a lifetime couldn't teach them
That back behind pursuit it couldn't reach them;
None flew behind me to be left alone.

Well, something for a snowstorm to have shown
The country's singing strength thus brought together,   50
That though repressed and moody with the weather
Was nonetheless there ready to be freed
And sing the wild flowers up from root and seed.

THE LOCKLESS DOOR

It went many years,
But at last came a knock,
And I thought of the door
With no lock to lock.

I blew out the light,   5
I tiptoed the floor,

And raised both hands
In prayer to the door.

But the knock came again.
My window was wide;   10
I climbed on the sill
And descended outside.

Back over the sill
I bade a "Come in"
To whatever the knock   15
At the door may have been.

So at a knock
I emptied my cage
To hide in the world
And alter with age.   20

THE NEED OF BEING VERSED
IN COUNTRY THINGS

The house had gone to bring again
To the midnight sky a sunset glow.
Now the chimney was all of the house that stood,
Like a pistil after the petals go.

The barn opposed across the way,   5
That would have joined the house in flame
Had it been the will of the wind, was left
To bear forsaken the place's name.

No more it opened with all one end
For teams that came by the stony road   10
To drum on the floor with scurrying hoofs

241

And brush the mow with the summer load.

The birds that came to it through the air
At broken windows flew out and in,
Their murmur more like the sigh we sigh   15
From too much dwelling on what has been.

Yet for them the lilac renewed its leaf,
And the aged elm, though touched with fire;
And the dry pump flung up an awkward arm;
And the fence post carried a strand of wire.   20

For them there was really nothing sad.
But though they rejoiced in the nest they kept,
One had to be versed in country things
Not to believe the phoebes wept.

West-Running Brook

: 1928 :

SPRING POOLS

These pools that, though in forests, still reflect
The total sky almost without defect,
And like the flowers beside them, chill and shiver,
Will like the flowers beside them soon be gone,
And yet not out by any brook or river,   5
But up by roots to bring dark foliage on.

The trees that have it in their pent-up buds
To darken nature and be summer woods—
Let them think twice before they use their powers
To blot out and drink up and sweep away   10
These flowery waters and these watery flowers
From snow that melted only yesterday.

THE FREEDOM OF THE MOON

I've tried the new moon tilted in the air
Above a hazy tree-and-farmhouse cluster
As you might try a jewel in your hair.
I've tried it fine with little breadth of luster,
Alone, or in one ornament combining   5
With one first-water star almost as shining.

I put it shining anywhere I please.
By walking slowly on some evening later
I've pulled it from a crate of crooked trees,
And brought it over glossy water, greater,   10
And dropped it in, and seen the image wallow,
The color run, all sorts of wonder follow.

245

THE ROSE FAMILY

The rose is a rose,
And was always a rose.
But the theory now goes
That the apple's a rose,
And the pear is, and so's   5
The plum, I suppose.
The dear only knows
What will next prove a rose.
You, of course, are a rose—
But were always a rose.   10

FIREFLIES IN THE GARDEN

Here come real stars to fill the upper skies,
And here on earth come emulating flies
That, though they never equal stars in size
(And they were never really stars at heart),
Achieve at times a very starlike start.   5
Only, of course, they can't sustain the part.

ATMOSPHERE

Inscription for a garden wall

Winds blow the open grassy places bleak;
But where this old wall burns a sunny cheek,
They eddy over it too toppling weak
To blow the earth or anything self-clear;
Moisture and color and odor thicken here.   5
The hours of daylight gather atmosphere.

DEVOTION

The heart can think of no devotion
Greater than being shore to the ocean—
Holding the curve of one position,
Counting an endless repetition.

ON GOING UNNOTICED

As vain to raise a voice as a sigh
In the tumult of free leaves on high.
What are you, in the shadow of trees
Engaged up there with the light and breeze?

Less than the coralroot, you know,   5
That is content with the daylight low,
And has no leaves at all of its own;
Whose spotted flowers hang meanly down.

You grasp the bark by a rugged pleat,
And look up small from the forest's feet.   10
The only leaf it drops goes wide,
Your name not written on either side.

You linger your little hour and are gone,
And still the woods sweep leafily on,
Not even missing the coralroot flower   15
You took as a trophy of the hour.

THE COCOON

As far as I can see, this autumn haze
That spreading in the evening air both ways
Makes the new moon look anything but new

247

And pours the elm-tree meadow full of blue,
Is all the smoke from one poor house alone,   5
With but one chimney it can call its own;
So close it will not light an early light,
Keeping its life so close and out of sight
No one for hours has set a foot outdoors
So much as to take care of evening chores.   10
The inmates may be lonely womenfolk.
I want to tell them that with all this smoke
They prudently are spinning their cocoon
And anchoring it to an earth and moon
From which no winter gale can hope to blow it—   15
Spinning their own cocoon did they but know it.

A PASSING GLIMPSE

To Ridgely Torrence
on last looking into his "Hesperides"

I often see flowers from a passing car
That are gone before I can tell what they are.

I want to get out of the train and go back
To see what they were beside the track.

I name all the flowers I am sure they weren't: 5
Not fireweed loving where woods have burnt—

Not bluebells gracing a tunnel mouth—
Not lupine living on sand and drouth.

Was something brushed across my mind
That no one on earth will ever find?   10

Heaven gives its glimpses only to those
Not in position to look too close.

A PECK OF GOLD

Dust always blowing about the town,
Except when sea fog laid it down,
And I was one of the children told
Some of the blowing dust was gold.

All the dust the wind blew high   5
Appeared like gold in the sunset sky,
But I was one of the children told
Some of the dust was really gold.

Such was life in the Golden Gate:
Gold dusted all we drank and ate,   10
And I was one of the children told,
"We all must eat our peck of gold."

ACCEPTANCE

When the spent sun throws up its rays on cloud
And goes down burning into the gulf below,
No voice in nature is heard to cry aloud
At what has happened. Birds, at least, must know
It is the change to darkness in the sky.   5
Murmuring something quiet in her breast,
One bird begins to close a faded eye;
Or overtaken too far from his nest,
Hurrying low above the grove, some waif
Swoops just in time to his remembered tree.   10
At most he thinks or twitters softly, "Safe!
Now let the night be dark for all of me.
Let the night be too dark for me to see
Into the future. Let what will be, be."

ONCE BY THE PACIFIC

The shattered water made a misty din.
Great waves looked over others coming in,
And thought of doing something to the shore
That water never did to land before.
The clouds were low and hairy in the skies,   5
Like locks blown forward in the gleam of eyes.
You could not tell, and yet it looked as if
The shore was lucky in being backed by cliff,
The cliff in being backed by continent;
It looked as if a night of dark intent   10
Was coming, and not only a night, an age.
Someone had better be prepared for rage.
There would be more than ocean-water broken
Before God's last *Put out the Light* was spoken.

LODGED

The rain to the wind said,
"You push and I'll pelt."
They so smote the garden bed
That the flowers actually knelt,
And lay lodged—though not dead.   5
I know how the flowers felt.

A MINOR BIRD

I have wished a bird would fly away,
And not sing by my house all day;

Have clapped my hands at him from the door
When it seemed as if I could bear no more.

250

The fault must partly have been in me.   5
The bird was not to blame for his key.

And of course there must be something wrong
In wanting to silence any song.

BEREFT

Where had I heard this wind before
Change like this to a deeper roar?
What would it take my standing there for,
Holding open a restive door,
Looking downhill to a frothy shore?   5
Summer was past and day was past.
Somber clouds in the west were massed.
Out in the porch's sagging floor
Leaves got up in a coil and hissed,
Blindly struck at my knee and missed.   10
Something sinister in the tone
Told me my secret must be known:
Word I was in the house alone
Somehow must have gotten abroad,
Word I was in my life alone,   15
Word I had no one left but God.

TREE AT MY WINDOW

Tree at my window, window tree,
My sash is lowered when night comes on;
But let there never be curtain drawn
Between you and me.

Vague dream-head lifted out of the ground,   5
And thing next most diffuse to cloud,

251

Not all your light tongues talking aloud
Could be profound.

But, tree, I have seen you taken and tossed,
And if you have seen me when I slept,   10
You have seen me when I was taken and swept
And all but lost.

That day she put our heads together,
Fate had her imagination about her,
Your head so much concerned with outer,   15
Mine with inner, weather.

THE PEACEFUL SHEPHERD

If heaven were to do again,
And on the pasture bars
I leaned to line the figures in
Between the dotted stars,

I should be tempted to forget,   5
I fear, the Crown of Rule,
The Scales of Trade, the Cross of Faith,
As hardly worth renewal.

For these have governed in our lives,
And see how men have warred.   10
The Cross, the Crown, the Scales may all
As well have been the Sword.

THE THATCH

Out alone in the winter rain,
Intent on giving and taking pain.

But never was I far out of sight
Of a certain upper-window light.
The light was what it was all about: 5
I would not go in till the light went out;
It would not go out till I came in.
Well, we should see which one would win,
We should see which one would be first to yield.
The world was a black invisible field.   10
The rain by rights was snow for cold.
The wind was another layer of mold.
But the strangest thing: in the thick old thatch,
Where summer birds had been given hatch,
Had fed in chorus, and lived to fledge,   15
Some still were living in hermitage.
And as I passed along the eaves
So low I brushed the straw with my sleeves,
I flushed birds out of hole after hole,
Into the darkness. It grieved my soul,   20
It started a grief within a grief,
To think their case was beyond relief—
They could not go flying about in search
Of their nest again, nor find a perch.
They must brood where they fell in mulch and mire, 25
Trusting feathers and inward fire
Till daylight made it safe for a flyer.
My greater grief was by so much reduced
As I thought of them without nest or roost.
That was how that grief started to melt.   30
They tell me the cottage where we dwelt,
Its wind-torn thatch goes now unmended;
Its life of hundreds of years has ended
By letting the rain I knew outdoors
In onto the upper chamber floors.   35

A WINTER EDEN

A winter garden in an alder swamp,
Where conies now come out to sun and romp,
As near a paradise as it can be
And not melt snow or start a dormant tree.

It lifts existence on a plane of snow   5
One level higher than the earth below,
One level nearer heaven overhead,
And last year's berries shining scarlet red.

It lifts a gaunt luxuriating beast
Where he can stretch and hold his highest feast   10
On some wild apple-tree's young tender bark,
What well may prove the year's high girdle mark.

So near to paradise all pairing ends:
Here loveless birds now flock as winter friends,
Content with bud-inspecting. They presume   15
To say which buds are leaf and which are bloom.

A feather-hammer gives a double knock.
This Eden day is done at two o'clock.
An hour of winter day might seem too short
To make it worth life's while to wake and sport.   20

THE FLOOD

Blood has been harder to dam back than water.
Just when we think we have it impounded safe
Behind new barrier walls (and let it chafe!),
It breaks away in some new kind of slaughter.
We choose to say it is let loose by the devil;   5
But power of blood itself releases blood.

254

It goes by might of being such a flood
Held high at so unnatural a level.
It will have outlet, brave and not so brave.
Weapons of war and implements of peace   10
Are but the points at which it finds release.
And now it is once more the tidal wave
That when it has swept by, leaves summits stained.
Oh, blood will out. It cannot be contained.

ACQUAINTED WITH THE NIGHT

I have been one acquainted with the night.
I have walked out in rain—and back in rain.
I have outwalked the furthest city light.

I have looked down the saddest city lane.
I have passed by the watchman on his beat   5
And dropped my eyes, unwilling to explain.

I have stood still and stopped the sound of feet
When far away an interrupted cry
Came over houses from another street,

But not to call me back or say good-by;   10
And further still at an unearthly height
One luminary clock against the sky

Proclaimed the time was neither wrong nor right.
I have been one acquainted with the night.

THE LOVELY SHALL BE CHOOSERS

The Voice said, "Hurl her down!"
The Voices, "How far down?"

"Seven levels of the world."

"How much time have we?"

"Take twenty years.   5
She *would* refuse love safe with wealth and honor!
The lovely shall be choosers, shall they?
Then let them choose!"

"Then we shall let her choose?"

"Yes, let her choose.   10
Take up the task beyond her choosing."

Invisible hands crowded on her shoulder
In readiness to weigh upon her.
But she stood straight still,
In broad round earrings, gold and jet with pearls,   15
And broad round suchlike brooch,
Her cheeks high-colored,
Proud and the pride of friends.

The Voice asked, "You can let her choose?"

"Yes, we can let her and still triumph."   20

"Do it by joys, and leave her always blameless.
Be her first joy her wedding,
That though a wedding,
Is yet—well, something they know, he and she.
And after that her next joy   25
That though she grieves, her grief is secret:
Those friends know nothing of her grief to make it shameful.
Her third joy that though now they cannot help but know,
They move in pleasure too far off
To think much or much care.   30
Give her a child at either knee for fourth joy

256

To tell once and once only, for them never to forget,
How once she walked in brightness,
And make them see it in the winter firelight.
But give her friends, for then she dare not tell   35
For their foregone incredulousness.
And be her next joy this:
Her never having deigned to tell them.
Make her among the humblest even
Seem to them less than they are.   40
Hopeless of being known for what she has been,
Failing of being loved for what she is,
Give her the comfort for her sixth of knowing
She fails from strangeness to a way of life
She came to from too high too late to learn.   45
Then send some *one* with eyes to see
And wonder at her where she is,
And words to wonder in her hearing how she came there,
But without time to linger for her story.
Be her last joy her heart's going out to this one   50
So that she almost speaks.
You know them—seven in all."

"Trust us," the Voices said.

WEST-RUNNING BROOK

"Fred, where is north?"

                    "North? North is there, my love.
The brook runs west."

                    "West-Running Brook then call it."
(West-Running Brook men call it to this day.)
"What does it think it's doing running west

257

When all the other country brooks flow east   5
To reach the ocean? It must be the brook
Can trust itself to go by contraries
The way I can with you—and you with me—
Because we're—we're—I don't know what we are.   9
What are we?"

        "Young or new?"

                      "We must be something.
We've said we two. Let's change that to we three.
As you and I are married to each other,
We'll both be married to the brook. We'll build
Our bridge across it, and the bridge shall be
Our arm thrown over it asleep beside it.   15
Look, look, it's waving to us with a wave
To let us know it hears me."

                  "Why, my dear,
That wave's been standing off this jut of shore—"
(The black stream, catching on a sunken rock,
Flung backward on itself in one white wave,   20
And the white water rode the black forever,
Not gaining but not losing, like a bird
White feathers from the struggle of whose breast
Flecked the dark stream and flecked the darker pool
Below the point, and were at last driven wrinkled   25
In a white scarf against the far-shore alders.)
"That wave's been standing off this jut of shore
Ever since rivers, I was going to say,
Were made in heaven. It wasn't waved to us."

"It wasn't, yet it was. If not to you,   30
It was to me—in an annunciation."

"Oh, if you take it off to lady-land,

As't were the country of the Amazons
We men must see you to the confines of
And leave you there, ourselves forbid to enter—   35
It is your brook! I have no more to say."

"Yes, you have, too. Go on. You thought of something."

"Speaking of contraries, see how the brook
In that white wave runs counter to itself.
It is from that in water we were from   40
Long, long before we were from any creature.
Here we, in our impatience of the steps,
Get back to the beginning of beginnings,
The stream of everything that runs away.
Some say existence like a Pirouot   45
And Pirouette, forever in one place,
Stands still and dances, but it runs away;
It seriously, sadly, runs away
To fill the abyss's void with emptiness.
It flows beside us in this water brook,   50
But it flows over us. It flows between us
To separate us for a panic moment.
It flows between us, over us, and *with* us.
And it is time, strength, tone, light, life, and love—
And even substance lapsing unsubstantial;   55
The universal cataract of death
That spends to nothingness—and unresisted,
Save by some strange resistance in itself,
Not just a swerving, but a throwing back,
As if regret were in it and were sacred.   60
It has this throwing backward on itself
So that the fall of most of it is always
Raising a little, sending up a little.
Our life runs down in sending up the clock.

259

The brook runs down in sending up our life.   65
The sun runs down in sending up the brook.
And there is something sending up the sun.
It is this backward motion toward the source,
Against the stream, that most we see ourselves in,
The tribute of the current to the source.   70
It is from this in nature we are from.
It is most us."

    "Today will be the day
You said so."

    "No, today will be the day
You said the brook was called West-Running Brook."

"Today will be the day of what we both said."   75

SAND DUNES

Sea waves are green and wet,
But up from where they die
Rise others vaster yet,
And those are brown and dry.

They are the sea made land   5
To come at the fisher town
And bury in solid sand
The men she could not drown.

She may know cove and cape,
But she does not know mankind   10
If by any change of shape
She hopes to cut off mind.

Men left her a ship to sink:
They can leave her a hut as well;

260

And be but more free to think   15
For the one more cast-off shell.

CANIS MAJOR

The great Overdog,
That heavenly beast
With a star in one eye,
Gives a leap in the east.

He dances upright   5
All the way to the west
And never once drops
On his forefeet to rest.

I'm a poor underdog,
But tonight I will bark   10
With the great Overdog
That romps through the dark.

A SOLDIER

He is that fallen lance that lies as hurled,
That lies unlifted now, come dew, come rust,
But still lies pointed as it plowed the dust.
If we who sight along it round the world,
See nothing worthy to have been its mark,   5
It is because like men we look too near,
Forgetting that as fitted to the sphere,
Our missiles always make too short an arc.
They fall, they rip the grass, they intersect
The curve of earth, and striking, break their own;   10
They make us cringe for metal-point on stone.
But this we know, the obstacle that checked

261

And tripped the body, shot the spirit on
Further than target ever showed or shone.

IMMIGRANTS

No ship of all that under sail or steam
Have gathered people to us more and more
But, Pilgrim-manned, the *Mayflower* in a dream
Has been her anxious convoy in to shore.

HANNIBAL

Was there ever a cause too lost,
Ever a cause that was lost too long,
Or that showed with the lapse of time too vain
For the generous tears of youth and song?

THE FLOWER BOAT

The fisherman's swapping a yarn for a yarn
Under the hand of the village barber,
And here in the angle of house and barn
His deep-sea dory has found a harbor.

At anchor she rides the sunny sod,   5
As full to the gunnel of flowers growing
As ever she turned her home with cod
From Georges Bank when winds were blowing.

And I judge from that Elysian freight
That all they ask is rougher weather,   10
And dory and master will sail by fate
To seek for the Happy Isles together.

THE TIMES TABLE

More than halfway up the pass
Was a spring with a broken drinking glass,
And whether the farmer drank or not
His mare was sure to observe the spot
By cramping the wheel on a water bar,   5
Turning her forehead with a star,
And straining her ribs for a monster sigh;
To which the farmer would make reply,
"A sigh for every so many breath,
And for every so many sigh a death.   10
That's what I always tell my wife
Is the multiplication table of life."
The saying may be ever so true;
But it's just the kind of a thing that you
Nor I nor nobody else may say,   15
Unless our purpose is doing harm,
And then I know of no better way
To close a road, abandon a farm,
Reduce the births of the human race,
And bring back nature in people's place.   20

THE INVESTMENT

Over back where they speak of life as staying
("You couldn't call it living, for it ain't"),
There was an old, old house renewed with paint,
And in it a piano loudly playing.

Out in the plowed ground in the cold a digger,   5
Among unearthed potatoes standing still,
Was counting winter dinners, one a hill,
With half an ear to the piano's vigor.

263

All that piano and new paint back there,
Was it some money suddenly come into?   10
Or some extravagance young love had been to?
Or old love on an impulse not to care—

Not to sink under being man and wife,
But get some color and music out of life?

THE LAST MOWING

There's a place called Faraway Meadow
We never shall mow in again,
Or such is the talk at the farmhouse:
The meadow is finished with men.
Then now is the chance for the flowers   5
That can't stand mowers and plowers.
It must be now, though, in season
Before the not mowing brings trees on,
Before trees, seeing the opening,
March into a shadowy claim.   10
The trees are all I'm afraid of,
That flowers can't bloom in the shade of;
It's no more men I'm afraid of;
The meadow is done with the tame.
The place for the moment is ours   15
For you, O tumultuous flowers,
To go to waste and go wild in,
All shapes and colors of flowers,
I needn't call you by name.

THE BIRTHPLACE

Here further up the mountain slope
Than there was ever any hope,

My father built, enclosed a spring,
Strung chains of wall round everything,
Subdued the growth of earth to grass,   5
And brought our various lives to pass.
A dozen girls and boys we were.
The mountain seemed to like the stir,
And made of us a little while—
With always something in her smile.   10
Today she wouldn't know our name.
(No girl's, of course, has stayed the same.)
The mountain pushed us off her knees.
And now her lap is full of trees.

THE DOOR IN THE DARK

In going from room to room in the dark
I reached out blindly to save my face,
But neglected, however lightly, to lace
My fingers and close my arms in an arc.
A slim door got in past my guard,   5
And hit me a blow in the head so hard
I had my native simile jarred.
So people and things don't pair anymore
With what they used to pair with before.

DUST IN THE EYES

If, as they say, some dust thrown in my eyes
Will keep my talk from getting overwise,
I'm not the one for putting off the proof.
Let it be overwhelming, off a roof
And round a corner, blizzard snow for dust,   5
And blind me to a standstill if it must.

265

SITTING BY A BUSH IN BROAD SUNLIGHT

When I spread out my hand here today,
I catch no more than a ray
To feel of between thumb and fingers;
No lasting effect of it lingers.

There was one time and only the one   5
When dust really took in the sun;
And from that one intake of fire
All creatures still warmly suspire.

And if men have watched a long time
And never seen sun-smitten slime   10
Again come to life and crawl off,
We must not be too ready to scoff.

God once declared He was true
And then took the veil and withdrew,
And remember how final a hush   15
Then descended of old on the bush.

God once spoke to people by name.
The sun once imparted its flame.
One impulse persists as our breath;
The other persists as our faith.   20

THE ARMFUL

For every parcel I stoop down to seize
I lose some other off my arms and knees,
And the whole pile is slipping, bottles, buns—
Extremes too hard to comprehend at once,
Yet nothing I should care to leave behind.   5

266

With all I have to hold with, hand and mind
And heart, if need be, I will do my best
To keep their building balanced at my breast.
I crouch down to prevent them as they fall;
Then sit down in the middle of them all.   10
I had to drop the armful in the road
And try to stack them in a better load.

WHAT FIFTY SAID

When I was young my teachers were the old.
I gave up fire for form till I was cold.
I suffered like a metal being cast.
I went to school to age to learn the past.

Now I am old my teachers are the young.   5
What can't be molded must be cracked and sprung.
I strain at lessons fit to start a suture.
I go to school to youth to learn the future.

RIDERS

The surest thing there is is we are riders,
And though none too successful at it, guiders,
Through everything presented, land and tide
And now the very air, of what we ride.

What is this talked-of mystery of birth   5
But being mounted bareback on the earth?
We can just see the infant up astride,
His small fist buried in the bushy hide.

There is our wildest mount—a headless horse.

But though it runs unbridled off its course,   10
And all our blandishments would seem defied,
We have ideas yet that we haven't tried.

ON LOOKING UP BY CHANCE
AT THE CONSTELLATIONS

You'll wait a long, long time for anything much
To happen in heaven beyond the floats of cloud
And the Northern Lights that run like tingling nerves.
The sun and moon get crossed, but they never touch,
Nor strike out fire from each other, nor crash out loud. 5
The planets seem to interfere in their curves,
But nothing ever happens, no harm is done.
We may as well go patiently on with our life,
And look elsewhere than to stars and moon and sun
For the shocks and changes we need to keep us sane. 10
It is true the longest drouth will end in rain,
The longest peace in China will end in strife.
Still it wouldn't reward the watcher to stay awake
In hopes of seeing the calm of heaven break
On his particular time and personal sight.   15
That calm seems certainly safe to last tonight.

THE BEAR

The bear puts both arms around the tree above her
And draws it down as if it were a lover
And its chokecherries lips to kiss good-by,
Then lets it snap back upright in the sky.
Her next step rocks a boulder on the wall   5
(She's making her cross-country in the fall).

Her great weight creaks the barbed wire in its staples
As she flings over and off down through the maples,
Leaving on one wire tooth a lock of hair.
Such is the uncaged progress of the bear. 10
The world has room to make a bear feel free;
The universe seems cramped to you and me.
Man acts more like the poor bear in a cage,
That all day fights a nervous inward rage,
His mood rejecting all his mind suggests. 15
He paces back and forth and never rests
The toenail click and shuffle of his feet,
The telescope at one end of his beat,
And at the other end the microscope,
Two instruments of nearly equal hope, 20
And in conjunction giving quite a spread.
Or if he rests from scientific tread,
'Tis only to sit back and sway his head
Through ninety-odd degrees of arc, it seems,
Between two metaphysical extremes. 25
He sits back on his fundamental butt
With lifted snout and eyes (if any) shut
(He almost looks religious but he's not),
And back and forth he sways from cheek to cheek,
At one extreme agreeing with one Greek, 30
At the other agreeing with another Greek,
Which may be thought, but only so to speak.
A baggy figure, equally pathetic
When sedentary and when peripatetic.

THE EGG AND THE MACHINE

He gave the solid rail a hateful kick.
From far away there came an answering tick,

269

And then another tick. He knew the code:
His hate had roused an engine up the road.
He wished when he had had the track alone   5
He had attacked it with a club or stone
And bent some rail wide open like a switch,
So as to wreck the engine in the ditch.
Too late though, now, he had himself to thank.
Its click was rising to a nearer clank.   10
Here it came breasting like a horse in skirts.
(He stood well back for fear of scalding squirts.)
Then for a moment all there was was size,
Confusion, and a roar that drowned the cries
He raised against the gods in the machine.   15
Then once again the sandbank lay serene.
The traveler's eye picked up a turtle trail,
Between the dotted feet a streak of tail,
And followed it to where he made out vague
But certain signs of buried turtle's egg;   20
And probing with one finger not too rough,
He found suspicious sand, and sure enough,
The pocket of a little turtle mine.
If there was one egg in it there were nine,
Torpedo-like, with shell of gritty leather,   25
All packed in sand to wait the trump together.
"You'd better not disturb me anymore,"
He told the distance, "I am armed for war.
The next machine that has the power to pass
Will get this plasm in its goggle glass."   30